PUBLIC RELATIONS
FOR
SCHOOL PERSONNEL

PUBLIC RELATIONS
FOR
SCHOOL PERSONNEL

FRANK MAYER

PENDELL
PUBLISHING
COMPANY

International Standard Book Number: 0-87812-072-6

Library of Congress Catalog Card Number: 74-76462

To Jan — a wonderful wife with patience and understanding.

CONTENTS

CHAPTER I

CHAPTER II

CHAPTER III

CHAPTER IV

CHAPTER V

CHAPTER VI

CHAPTER VII

CHAPTER VIII

CHAPTER IX

CHAPTER X

CHAPTER XI

CONTENTS (Cont'd)

LIST OF FIGURES

INTRODUCTION

This book has been written to serve as a guideline for those school officials who want to develop a planned public relations program. Such a program requires the efforts of all those involved in a school operation. Therefore, included in this book are ideas and suggestions for students, teachers, principals, superintendents, central office staff, board of education members and community leaders. The publication is authored by a practicing superintendent of schools who has been responsible for public relations programs in both small and medium-sized school communities. The book is light on theory, but heavy on the everyday techniques and practices involved in an effective public relations program. It is a basic "nuts and bolts" approach to school-county relations.

Public relations exist in every school district whether school officials are aware of them or not; whether school officials want them or not. In the absence of a planned public relations program, the unplanned public relations will be haphazard, disorganized and riddled with misinformation. Students, staff and parents will disseminate upon the community a flow of subjective information, much of which may be prejudiced or inaccurate.

An effective public relations program will present accurate school facts and information. In the absence of a planned program, inaccurate information and biased opinions will abound in the community.

School administrators must realize that effective public relations skills are necessary not only to function well as educational leaders but also for the benefit of their own professional future. Studies have shown that when administrators are released from employment that one of the main causes for such releases is difficulty in working with the community and relating to citizens.

The need to explain school programs has increased since World War II. Prior to that time, changes in the public schools were minimal and slow. There was little difference between schools attended by students and those attended by their parents. Since World War II, however, changes in public education have been rapid — especially in the areas of organization, curriculum, and methodology. Many adults do not understand how today's schools operate. When people don't understand, they become suspicious, confused, and often critical. Therefore, an effective school information program is needed to help citizens to comprehend today's school operation. Unless they do understand, support will be lacking and school progress and change will be thwarted.

Citizens today are more aware and concerned of the cost of operating public schools; many know that schools require the greatest share of the local property tax receipts; that schools receive a large share of the state tax revenue. Therefore, they are demanding more information about how tax dollars are being spent and the services they are receiving.

Today's citizens are accustomed to receiving well-written periodic reports; they expect to be informed. They have been conditioned to such service through the advertising programs developed by business and industry which have done an excellent job of keeping customers and stockholders informed.

As school districts grow in size due to new housing or consolidations, citizens feel more removed or distant from their schools; they are more distant geographically and in spirit. In order to reduce this void, school officials must develop new ties and lines of communication with their constituents.

This book is designed to provide guidelines for developing techniques and practices which can be used to build a wholesome relationship between the school and community.

CHAPTER I

**PUBLIC RELATIONS —
SOME BASIC PRINCIPLES**

PUBLIC RELATIONS —
SOME BASIC PRINCIPLES

In this first chapter, the basic principles of a strong balanced school-community program are presented. Before a district can enjoy an effective public relations program it must have its house in order: there must be harmonious working relations among staff members and moral must be good; there must be a public relations-minded administrative staff and board of education; a strong educational program must exist. With such a base firmly established, the tools of public relations can be developed which lead to effective newsletters, radio broadcasts, community seminars and opinion polling.

THE COMMUNICATIONS PROCESS

Communications are classified in the following manner:

One-way

Feedback

Two-way

"One-way" refers to communications efforts or products which originate at the school and are for community or staff consumption. They travel from the school to the recipient with no opportunity provided for the return of information to the school. Examples of one-way efforts are newsletters, radio broadcasts and speakers.

"Feedback" refers to the community's reactions to the school program — thoughts, opinions, reactions, and evaluations of the educational program of members of the various publics which make up the community. A community questionnaire, for example, will provide the school staff with "feedback."

"Two-way" communications result in information flowing to an audience (community) as well as providing a return of information. A parent conference for example, provides two-way communication: the teacher gives information and receives information from the parent.

When a district develops its first planned public relations program, its initial products are usually the "one-way" media because school people are most familiar and feel more competent and comfortable with them. They are easier to produce than those utilizing feedback techniques and allow the novice public relations technicians time to gain experience and confidence. However, public relations personnel in many districts devote a disproportionate amount of time to the "one-way" media. About as much time and effort should be allowed for feedback techniques as is allowed for one-way methods.

Although a school may send out reams of one-way communications, no one will ever know how many citizens actually receive and read the messages. No one will know their reactions. There is no way to evaluate the effectiveness of a one-way program.

A YEAR-ROUND PROGRAM

The school public relations program must be a continuous activity. It will not be effective if it is turned on just prior to an election in order to help pass a bond issue or levy and then turned off or down after passage. Sporadic public relations are not acceptable in today's society. School officials must maintain such a constant program that when a school issue is on the ballot, passage requires only an acceleration of normal public relations.

BEDROCK

Three important ingredients are required for an effective school public relations program:

1. A public relations oriented board of education,

2. A board-adopted policy on public relations,

3. A strong educational program.

Members of the board of education must be public relations oriented and must be willing to support a public relations program with enthusiasm and dollars. An adopted policy on school-community relations, containing the basic public relations principles for which it stands, should be adopted by the board. Such a policy is a pledge from the board to support and work for an effective public relations program. An example of a public relations policy developed by Beverly Hills Unified School District is shown in Figure 1.

Equally important as the board-adopted policy is a strong educational program for the schools. A cliche, "Operate a good school program and you have the 'cornerstone' of a good public relations program," is often used by school-community personnel. A sound educational program emanates positive public relations. The board must structure its policies and base its decisions on the premise of a strong educational program for its schools.

PRIORITIES

If the school's basic educational program is weak, the administration and board must give priority to building and strengthening the program. First, the school program must be improved to provide the needed foundation for public relations. Then time and energy can be channeled to develop an effective school-community program.

An effective program requires that a school have a staff with harmonious working relationships. The school must first have its "house in order" to have an effective external public relations program. If employees lack an "esprit de corps," the administration must first

GENERAL PUBLIC RELATIONS POLICY

Public relations policy shall be to establish in the minds of the various publics through actions and communications that the Beverly Hills Unified School District...

... Is a system of education that is second to no other in the country.

... Serves in the best interests of students, district personnel, parents, and taxpayers, and recognizes its responsibility to the community, state, and the nation.

... Realizes it must continually endeavor to develop a program of education that will challenge all students to achieve to the maximum of their abilities.

... Recognizes that school expenditures shall be consistent with sound principles of education and public finance.

... Strives to improve human relations in contacts with all its publics, to heed their opinions, and to keep them informed to deserve and build good will, understanding, and confidence.

It shall be the objective of the public relations program to make and hold friends for Beverly Hills Unified School District through development of a "two-way street of communication" with all its "publics" — student, teacher, classified personnel, parent, resident, supplier. Emphasis in the public relations program will be on "information," not "persuasion." Public relations also shall advance the education program by aiding in the development of a high morale in an informed and concerned classified personnel and faculty, which will continually set high standards of achievement for themselves and for their students.

It shall be the responsibility of the supervisor of information, under the direction of the Superintendent, to develop and execute public relations and publicity programs to meet these objectives. He shall have sole responsibility for dissemination of all information concerning the district, its programs, and its personnel. This also pertains to material written by other school personnel for all media — press, radio, television, and periodicals, both lay and professional.

Figure 1 — Public Relations Policy

---

direct its efforts inwardly to correct the situation before the outward efforts to the community can be effective.

The following practices help build such an "esprit de corps":

A staff receives maximum school information. For example, the staff receives copies of important news releases such as the hiring of the new principal or superintendent before it is announced by the news media.

A staff is allowed input on decisions which affect them. For example, when the board develops a policy on staff evaluation, teacher representatives are invited to help develop the policy.

6

Administrators take a personal interest in staff members. For example, if a teacher's child breaks an arm, the principal volunteers to take his class so he can be with his child.

One high school principal built esprit de corps by having miniature board of directors meetings with teachers every period of the day once a month. In small groups of ten or twelve, teachers were made to feel like executives who could help the principal solve problems and did. These replaced one monthly faculty meeting of 80 teachers.

He gave the same executive treatment to representative students whom he invited to lunch with him in the home economics room. At the end of the year he took especially helpful students to a restaurant for dinner, three or four at a time. Ideas and cooperation stemmed from this VIP treatment.

THE MOST EFFECTIVE PUBLICITY AGENTS

The most effective, important and numerous public relations agents available to the school are the children. These vehicles are loved, respected, cherished and accepted in most families. They are an omnipresent avenue into each home. Many accept their utterings about the school as the gospel truth. If the child's version of an incident conflicts with that of a teacher's, the parents usually believe the child.

Children are ever-flowing fountains of school information to the homes and to the community over which the school has little control or knowledge. The publicity, good and bad, correct and incorrect, objective or biased, is disseminated to the family, friends, relatives and neighborhood.

Since students are the school's most effective publicity agents, is there anything that can be done to nurture them in this important role? An educational program which challenges all pupils will produce students with positive attitudes. If the school has as its goal "to educate all of its students to the maximum of their ability," teachers must be concerned that the pupils will reflect this success in the home and in the community. Such a program should develop students who are happy and enthused about school; positive reports of the school will result.

THE WHOLE SCHOOL STORY

A well-balanced public relations program must mirror a true picture of the district. It must display accomplishments as well as the problems of the school. Presenting only the "positive picture" of the schools is short-sighted. Such an approach makes teachers and administrators look competent and avoids community criticism, but only temporarily.

By presenting the total school story, difficulties as well as accomplishments, unpleasant incidents as well as pleasant ones, the community is better prepared when bigger problems such as a deficit budget or loss of accrediting occurs.

Telling only the positive story leads citizens to believe that their schools are fine as they are. Reacting to the authors first three newsletters, an alert PTA member criticized, "You present only the good things! Why don't you use some space for your problems?" She suggested, "Reserve a portion of every newsletter for information which describes district problems." After that, a portion of each edition was reserved for local school problems.

By describing the inadequacies of the educational program, educators plant the seed for some of the public to say "Our schools need to improve; and to improve they need money." An informed public will be better prepared than a sheltered public when problems and needs are brought to light.

REACHING THE COMMUNITY WITH A MULTIPHASIC PUBLIC RELATIONS EFFORT

Many avenues of communication are available to reach members of the community, but many organizations (commercial, business, institutional) are exploiting these avenues. All are competing for the attention of the school citizens. Messages are sprung at people through the mass media of radio, television, newspapers and magazines. The most clever and original message gets the attention of the citizens. The average person is deluged with mail, some personally addressed but much of it "junk mail" which may be discarded without even a glance at its contents. The school must not just join the competitive battle of communications; it must achieve success in the struggle. School people, too, must be creative and original.

The typical school community is composed of many separate groups or "publics." A few of them, typical of most communities, include ethnic groups, businessmen, laborers, farmers, professionals, intelligentsia, veterans, service organizations, senior citizens, political and religious groups. Even an array of communication tools cannot reach all of these publics. A few community groups insulate themselves and defy almost all means of communication — they avoid radio, newspapers and community meetings. Many times communication with such groups can take place only by home visits made by the teacher or principal.

Communication problems are further complicated because communities and schools are bigger and more complex than ever before. Many of the inhabitants use the district as a bedroom community — they work, spend most of their money and have interests away from the area. Therefore, they lack community interests; they do not participate, and this widens the distance between the public and the school.

At one time communities were rather homogeneous in population make-up and contained people with similar backgrounds and values. These have given way to "mixed populations," containing people with divergent backgrounds, interests and values. A mixed community has persons with great variations in the values they hold for education. If some of these groups polarize, the board of education and the superintendent may be caught in the middle of a "tug of values."

Because of the complex population found in most communities, a "multi phasic approach" to communications is proposed. The school must develop a diversified set of public relations tools, each designed to reach a specific part of the public. Every known avenue of communication must be exploited. By using many media, the school message can reach a maximum number of the citizens.

THE HUMAN TOUCH

Public relations programs can be more effective if there is more of a "human touch." Although a comprehensive public relations program can be most sophisticated, it can also be cold and lifeless without a certain amount of human involvement. Face-to-face, person-to-person contact is the most effective "two-way" method of communicating.

BELL STUDY

A study of supervisory-employee relations was conducted by the Illinois Bell Telephone Company to determine the effectiveness of face-to-face internal communications. The study, which parallels principal-teacher relationships, indicated slightly better than one-half of all employees would have liked more information from their supervisor, and about one-fourth felt that their supervisor rarely or never discussed the company and its operations except for job related material. About one-fifth of all employees indicated they rarely or never had a chance to ask questions of their supervisor.

Bell employees gave the highest ratings for communications which involve (1) face-to-face talk with the supervisor and (2) group meetings.

As business and schools become larger and more complex in operation, too many supervisors and principals lose a part of the art of staff communication.

Morton Knapp, Assistant Vice President for Bell public relations, stated, "We have found ourselves in the business persuading supervisors that it's to their own self-interest to talk to their people. We have found ourselves having to sell at all levels of management the idea not only that the company can afford the considerable time it takes for two-way discussions, but that the company cannot really afford not to take the time."

Public relations activities which are personal and face-to-face, such as kaffee klatsches and luncheons with community leaders, do not reach large numbers of people and are very time consuming. Therefore, many administrators minimize such contacts. A balance, however, must be struck between the printed, lifeless media and the personal, face-to-face, word-of-mouth techniques.

CITIZEN INVOLVEMENT

Second in effectiveness to direct personal contact is citizen involvement in school activities and projects. As a general rule, the more adult involvement, the greater the community understanding and support for education — provided parents are involved in proper assignments. The effectiveness of the public relations program will increase proportionately to the percentage of citizens meaningfully involved in activities such as PTA councils, citizens' committees, public relations committees, and parent volunteers.

Being involved enables the citizens to have direct experiences which are more meaningful than vicarious experiences. The parents who become volunteer librarians or who are room mothers will develop a closeness to the school which will produce a better understanding and support of the school and its problems. They become effective disciples in the community.

Involvement has a corollary. Parents who observe a poorly organized school will become critical disciples in the community.

Increased parent involvement, when properly utilized, will forge stronger school-community bonds.

WARMTH IN COMMUNICATION

Teachers and administrators must guard against communications which are formal, stiff or cold. Some persons are sensitive to short demanding messages and may interpret unintended innuendos. For example, a teacher may write on the portion of the report card reserved for teachers' comments, "Parent conference needed." A more personal message, one with more warmth would be written "Dear Parent, a parent conference would be very valuable for Kathy. Won't you please call and make an appointment?" As another example, the principal may have the school secretary relay a message to the music teacher, "Stop at the principal's office." It would be a warmer message, however, if the relayed message were, "The principal would like you to stop at his office to arrange for an ensemble request." A short, curt message from the principal may cause a worrisome teacher to have a discomforting feeling. "What did I do now? Is there something wrong?" The message with a human touch is worthy of the extra effort involved.

LISTENING SKILLS

All school personnel can improve their "listening skills;" staff members must be willing to "hear people out." Everyone is anxious to present his problems and biases — but less anxious to listen to the problems of others. All employees should develop the ability to "listen with interest and understanding" because what a person is relaying in conversation is of great concern to him. The school person who dominates a one-to-one dialogue or a group conference, may not allow the other participant to fully express or vent his feelings. An unheard parent may be frustrated and embittered, and the school person may lose because he never heard the parent's message.

OPEÑ DOOR POLICY

The superintendent and his administrative staff should always maintain an "open door" policy and be willing to talk with staff members, parents and the general public. Full respect must be shown for each person's problems. If administrators are not readily available, they will be accused of isolating themselves, or placing themselves on a pedestal. Staff members must be encouraged to first present their problems and grievances to their immediate supervisors. However, if satisfaction is not received there, they must be heard by the next echelon and, finally, the superintendent.

COMMUNICATING WITH THE PUBLIC

Staff members must never become caustic or arrogant when working with parents. Citizens are the stockholders of the school organization; they are also the customers the school must serve. An iron-clad policy for good business operation is, "You don't argue with the customers!" Staff members must guard against being drawn into arguments or heated discussions with parents. When a staff member becomes insulting or caustic to a customer (the parent) he is automatically in the wrong.

When talking with, or writing for, the lay public, educators must guard against the use of pedagogical language. Staff members must write and speak so they can be understood by the general public. Parents are often reluctant to admit that they don't understand.

Sometimes they are afraid to ask questions that may make them seem uninformed. Although the level of communications will vary, depending on the sophistication of the audience, a safe rule-of-thumb is to use sixth-grade level language in writing or speaking to the general public.

The community composed largely of professional or high-income families will usually demand sophisticated, polished and well-written communications such as newsletters and annual reports. Lower-income areas, however, would disdain publications which appear to be expensive. The school message must be written in language best accepted and understood by the respective school community. Figure 2 presents a copy of campaign literature which probably would be accepted by members of a lower-income community but would not be well received in a higher income area.

RESPONDING TO PARENT CRITICISM

The ability to field public criticism with poise and diplomacy is an art. When a parent places a complaint, it is wrong for the administrator or teacher to become defensive, justify the school's position, cut the parent off, or classify him as a maverick. The public relations oriented staff member patiently and courteously hears a parent's criticism and either makes corrections based on the complaint or explains the school's position. For example, if a parent wants to know why teachers aren't using phonics to teach reading to her second-grade child, the administrator must courteously allow her to express herself without being defensive. Assuming that phonics are being taught, he must then follow with a verbal explanation of the school's position. In addition, he can show the parent a copy of the teachers' guide and indicate how the guide provides instruction on using phonics. Better still, the parent may be invited to visit a class in reading to observe the use of phonics in the reading instruction.

A parent requested door-to-door school bus service for youngsters living on her street because of heavy, high-speed traffic. Although board policy permitted door-to-door pickup on hazardous streets, the bus supervisor and superintendent didn't classify the area as dangerous. Instead of merely sending a letter of denial, the superintendent asked the local police and the bus supervisor to appear at the location, count cars and estimate car speeds on three different days. A report which

Pay · Go · Save · Dough

(1) *What's this P.A.Y. GO stuff?*

(1) It stands for *Pay As You Go*. It really is a tax levy for permanent improvement for the Springfield Schools.

(2) *Whose idea is this?*

(2) It's not new. Many city, village, and local school districts throughout Ohio use this method of financing their building programs rather than the traditional method.

(3) *What do you mean "traditional method?"*

(3) This is the most common method of paying for school buildings and grounds. It involves getting the voters' permission to issue bonds in order to raise money to build, remodel or purchase land.

(4) *What's wrong with that?*

(4) When bonds are issued, interest must be paid. Usually, this interest amounts to more than a third of the original principal. It works similar to buying a home with a 20 year mortgage — the interest is oppressive.

(5) *How is P.A.Y.GO different?*

(5) Money is collected on an annual basis and invested until needed. Interest is *collected* rather than *paid*.

– THIS SOUNDS GOOD – HOW CAN WE GET IT?

Act · Vote · Save · Now!

Figure 2 – Sample of Campaign Literature

indicated light traffic and reasonable speeds was mailed to each parent in the disputed area. The parents involved were very appreciative of the school's thorough investigation; no additional complaints were received.

A comprehensive study of each parent complaint is very time consuming. The investment of additional time and energy to study parent complaints, however, can pay handsome dividends. An arrogant rebuff of a disgruntled parent can produce waves of negative public relations in a community. Dissatisfied and angry parents can destroy school support. A questioning parent is as sincere about his position as the school official is of his. The parent deserves respect, patience and an explanation of the school's position.

VISIBILITY

The effective school administrator manages to get around his school and community; he is "visible" to his constituents. President Eisenhower made an effort to be visible when he flew to Korea to observe the war, first hand — a trip which affected the morale of U. S. troops and citizens.

The building principal cannot afford to spend all of his time cloistered in an office. This is a temptation because there is always something to do and, for many, it is an easier task to shuffle papers than to have person-to-person contacts. The effective principal must spend time in his community, at the PTA executive meeting, with teachers, students, cafeteria and custodial people. The superintendent should, occasionally, have lunch with a faculty, visit at a faculty meeting, talk with employees at the bus garage, maintenance shop and, of course, be as active as possible in the community.

PREPARING STUDENTS TO SUPPORT EDUCATION

Public school students are potential voters who will either support or oppose school issues. They must be educated while in school to the importance of good public schools. Many schools fail in this important responsibility. Too many students graduate after twelve years of social studies instruction and vote against public education when they visit the polls. They have not been taught to realize the important role that public education plays in our society.

All teachers in grades one to twelve are charged with the responsibility of teaching the importance of public education as a cornerstone of our society. The method used to introduce the concept, the method used to develop correct attitudes toward public education, will vary from teacher to teacher. Each educator, however, has the responsibility to teach the facts and offer the experiences which will lead to an understanding of the importance that the public school plays in our society — politically, economically and socially.

In addition to stressing the value of education at all levels, units on public school education should be taught in depth in grade eight or nine — prior to the drop-out age; and again in a senior high social studies class — prior to graduation. The "in-depth units" should be taught with the help of resource people who are available — the principal, superintendent or board members.

The classroom teacher has a vital role to play in educating students to the importance of education as the foundation of American democracy. The public school administrator has an even more important role — to encourage such instruction on all levels. The administrator who insists on such instruction is fulfilling his obligations to society and to education!

CHAPTER II

**ORGANIZING
A PUBLIC RELATIONS PROGRAM**

ORGANIZING A
PUBLIC RELATIONS PROGRAM

A board of education wishes to establish a public relations program or to increase the effectiveness of the present program. How does it go about such a task? Much of the success of a public relations effort depends on how sincere the board and superintendent are in wanting to improve the program; the attitude and enthusiasm of these leaders will determine the degree of success for the program.

The board must first develop a policy statement related to its position on public relations. Such a statement will contain goals such as:

Keeping the staff and community fully informed

Obtaining community feedback

Involvement of citizens in the school operation

Considering public opinion before making decisions

Periodic evaluation of the public relations program

A model policy statement is found in Chapter 1, Figure 1.

WHEN FUNDS ARE LACKING

Some school districts lack an adequate financial base and are chronically short of funds. School officials from such districts have been known to use the lack of funds for an excuse not to have a school-community program.

A public relations program need not cost a great deal of money. A fairly effective program can be developed with little or no financial expenditure. A public relations program need not be a replica of a sophisticated metropolitan district's program. Publications, for example, do not have to be slick four-colored productions. If funds are lacking, it is better to distribute a mimeographed community newsletter through elementary students than to have none at all.

One school district, which was short of funds, distributed a publication financed by a milk company as a public service. Although not a desirable way to finance the publication, it was better than no publication at all. Many public relations efforts such as kaffee klatsches, parent conferences, news releases, and radio appearances cost no money at all.

A small Wisconsin district developed a public relations program on approximately $200 a year. The Marshall school district, with a population of approximately 700 students, developed a program on this amount. The funds were used for postage, polaroid film, stationery and supplies for a spirit duplicator. A staff member who had interest and ability in journalism and who enjoyed working with people was given two class periods a week for the job. Every week he had the services of a secretary for one hour and student volunteers for three hours. Students served as typists, photographers, and reporters.

THE ROLE OF THE SUPERINTENDENT

The person most responsible for building an effective public relations program is the superintendent. In a small district, the superintendent serves as his own public relations specialist. In a large district, a staff member is appointed for the public relations assignment; yet the superintendent is still responsible. The superintendent must work closely with his public relations person to make sure the program is effective and stays abreast with rapidly changing values and technology.

Because the superintendent has the final say on budget development, he determines the magnitude of the public relations program: a full-time versus part-time specialist; a weekly staff newsletter or a monthly one; a monthly community newsletter versus a quarterly publication; an extensive observation of American Education Week versus a token program; a part-time photographer; attendance at public relations workshops.

The superintendent also sets the tone and example for his district and staff by his own community relations. He should accept citizen complaints with courtesy and patience and receive citizens with warmth and courtesy at school functions. His staff and community publications should be well written and be of excellent design. He should balance his written communications with person-to-person contacts and encourage his staff to develop good school-community relations. He should organize workshops to help the staff develop public relations and continually encourage them to use and develop these skills. He should encourage community use of school buildings and community involvement in school operations.

The Superintendent's role in public relations was well stated by Clayton Rose, a public relations consultant formerly with the New York State Teachers Association:

"Without question, the one person who has major responsibility for the PR program is the school's chief administrative officer — the superintendent of schools. It is his responsibility to guide, counsel, and recommend as the board of education moves toward the adoption of its policy on the school's PR. It is his responsibility to implement policy with a planned program. It is his responsibility to provide the leadership to set the program in motion.

It is his responsibility to recognize and utilize the talents of all members of the professional staff in carrying out the PR function. It is equally important that he delegate authority with responsibility and that he give credit where due for achievements and accomplishments."

GETTING STARTED

A logical way to begin a planned public relations program is to evaluate the existent public relations program — to compare the present program with the goals established by the board of education. This is called a needs assessment. Such an assessment can be conducted by an appointed public relations advisory committee. Representative teachers, citizens and students should be included in such a committee. Opinions of the public relations program should be solicited from staff, community residents, and students through interviews or through a questionnaire.

An evaluation can also be conducted by a professional counseling firm.

The new public relations specialist must first become acquainted with the school staff and the community. He must visit with representatives of the news media to determine how effectively school news is forwarded to them. He needs to identify and meet the business and industrial leaders, representatives of government and members of the community power structure. Techniques in working with such representatives follow in other chapters of this book.

The public relations specialist should visit other school public relations personnel in his area to solicit suggestions on getting started. He may wish to encourage his peers to meet periodically to exchange ideas. In addition to getting public relations ideas for his own district, he should obtain information on equipment and supplies needed to operate an effective operation. Typical equipment used in the public relations office includes an offset printer, addressing equipment, collator, photo enlarger, headliner. Since such equipment is expensive, the public relations director must work with his immediate supervisor to request budgeting of funds. For each request, the specialist should prepare a written justification and should obtain samples of the product obtainable with the equipment.

The newly appointed specialist should read texts in school public relations and periodic publications produced by the National School Public Relations Association (NSPRA) and attend the next public relations workshop offered by the American Association of School Administrators' National Academy, NSPRA, or School Management Institute in Columbus, Ohio.

The following activities are suggested for a modest first-year public relations program. It is better to have a limited program done right than to sponsor too many activities of a mediocre quality.

Publicize the board-adopted policy on public relations. The statement will make clear the board's position and desire for an effective public relations program.

Publicize board of education meetings widely and encourage the public to attend. Those in attendance should be given a copy of the agenda and should be given an opportunity to address the board if they wish.

Invite community organizations to send a representative to the board meeting.

A summary of the board meeting should be available to the staff and interested citizens the day after the meeting.

Develop a staff newsletter for periodic distribution.

Develop a community newsletter for periodic distribution.

Organize an effective citizens' committee.

The above list isn't magical. For the part-time specialist, it could be too much for one year. Each newly appointed specialist will want to review the many opportunities available to him and develop his own first-year listing of activities.

THE PUBLIC RELATIONS ADMINISTRATOR

In many school districts, especially those small in size, the superintendent must double for the public relations specialist. In districts where student enrollment exceeds 5,000, a school-community specialist may be employed either part-time or full-time. There are many titles used to designate the public relations specialist: Public Relations Director, Community Relations Coordinator, School Information Coordinator, Research Director. The position of school public relations specialist often draws community criticism. A common citizen lament is: "Why is our tax money being wasted on a person in this position? The money should be used for supplies and equipment." Parents liken the assignment to that of an advertising agent in business and many still don't understand the need of school public relations to improve the educational program. Such critics must be educated to the fact that any public institution dependent on community tax support must have a continuous public relations program if it wishes to remain effective and grow.

To avoid community criticism, some schools conceal the public relations specialist under a title such as Director of Research, although he may devote only 20% of his time to research and 80% to public relations.

Other schools avoid a direct public relations assignment completely. Their philosophy is that every school employee must be a public relations expert and that the most effective program will result if each member of the staff plays a role in the program. Dr. Arthur H. Rice, former editor of *Nation's Schools,* states, "The best evidence that good school-community relations is operating is the harmonious and cooperative school district where the efforts at public relations are not obvious — and where the public seems to know and understand, without being pressured!"

DUTIES OF THE PUBLIC RELATIONS ADMINISTRATOR

What does the public relations man do? *School Management Magazine* editors interviewed 15 top public relations people on the national level to obtain answers to this question. According to the panel, in addition to doing what is expected of every public relations director — newsletters, publications, answering citizens' questions, working with the news media, a public relations person must also:

- Advise and consult with the administrators as to the concerns of the staff and community.

- Organize special school programs such as dedications of buildings.

- Serve as a resource person for PTA's.

- Speak to civic organizations.

- Keep abreast of new public relations developments through membership in and participation in professional meetings.

— Promote school levy and bond issue campaigns.

The public relations director or the public relations department may, in addition be involved in all or a portion of the assignments listed below:

1. Preparing press, radio and television releases

2. Providing editorial services for central office publications

3. Establishing a speakers' bureau

4. Providing a standardized form for releasing news reports

5. Providing encouragement and assistance in public relations to all personnel

6. Maintaining a file on all releases

7. Maintaining a file on all published releases

8. Designing in-service programs in public relations

9. Serving as a resource person for school programs involving the community — open house, school building dedications.

10. Evaluating the district's public relations program.

Results of a public relations survey indicated that 90% of the full-time directors "considered press, radio and television contacts as one of their major responsibilities." They considered "editorial services" for the central office a minor assignment.

THE PUBLIC RELATIONS ADMINISTRATOR — A PROFILE

The Educational Research Service, which was at one time jointly sponsored by the National Education Association (NEA) and the American Association of School Administrators (AASA), has published several surveys on the public relations administrator. Results obtained from representative samplings indicated that most schools with enrollments of 50,000 or more employ a full-time public relations administrator.

Other significant results pertaining to full-time public relations personnel include:

1. 85-90% of public relations administrators report directly to the superintendent; others reported to the assistant superintendent or lesser administrative official.

2. Approximately 10% of the full-time directors were employed less than a full year.

3. About 60% of the positions require a bachelor's degree and 35% a master's degree. More than half of the respondents had master's degrees and several had doctorates.

4. Approximately 80% of the directors were men. Almost one-half were 40 years of age or under.

5. In the larger systems, most public relations directors have at least a secretary and one writer-editor.

6. Approximately 90% had a staff newsletter, but only 60% had a regular community newsletter.

COMMUNICATIONS

Communication is an essential aspect of most public relations activities. The *School Management* panel viewed the public relations man as a sort of "pivotal person or hub through which all communications, internal and external, flow. . . .They saw the public relations man as the disseminator of information going out from the school to its many publics — and the channel through which feedback from the community is returned to the school administration. Within the school system, his function is to keep each interest group — the board, superintendent, principals, teachers, staff and, yes, the students — tuned in to what all the others are doing and thinking.

"While this function is generally referred to as 'two-way communication,' the PR man's responsibility is much more than two-way. On some issues, he may need to inform as many as 20 or more different groups in terms that each will understand. Membership in groups overlap; for example, parents are also taxpayers and/or voters. So, a PR

28

director may be sending and receiving on a number of channels simultaneously, while continually passing along the views of one group to another in order to help them gain greater mutual understanding.

"Doing an effective job alone is impossible. One measure of the PR man's success, in the opinion of those who play the game, is the extent to which he can 'develop sensitivity of all employees in the system to ways in which they can aid the district's public relations program.' "

MULTIPLE PUBLIC RELATIONS EFFORTS

Communities are more heterogeneous than ever before and contain many publics: parents, nonparents, students, professionals, businessmen, craftsmen, laborers, senior citizens, ethnics, veterans, whites, nonwhites, just to mention a few. A particular public relations effort or tool will not reach all publics, and special techniques and media need to be developed to reach special groups. A "Gold Card Club," for example, will reach senior citizens; a Business-Industry-Education Council will result in contacts with businessmen; active membership in the Chamber of Commerce will lead to contacts with business leaders.

BALANCE

The public relations specialist must maintain a balance in his efforts — between the printed media and the person-to-person contacts. Printed materials are tangible and easy to crank out and they reach a multitude of persons, but are only "one-way" communications efforts. Person-to-person contacts involve much fewer people, are more time consuming and the effects are often intangible, but "two-way" communications do result.

The beginning public relations person usually will give a disproportional amount of time and effort to publications rather than to person-to-person efforts. A proper balance between the two efforts is important.

PUBLIC RELATIONS SPECIALIST'S BACKGROUND

What training should a person assigned to the school public relations position have? Should he have classroom experience? Is a journalism background a necessity? Should he have experience in business and industrial public relations? There is disagreement among educators on the answers to these questions.

Stanley Elam, editor of *Phi Delta Kappa Magazine,* believes that the public relations specialist should have experience in public education. He questions, "What defense do we have against an under-educated education writer educating half a million newspaper readers?" An opposite opinion is rendered by *Newsweek* education editor, Peter Janson, who opines that "A good education reporter must first be a good journalist."

Although school public relations personnel come from a variety of backgrounds — educational, journalism, business and industry — most of them were formerly employed by the public schools and have had classroom experience. Many have taught English or journalism. Art teachers, because of their creative talent and layout ability, are often selected for the role.

What type of person or personality will make the best public relations practitioner? According to Thomas Koerner, the individual should be congenial, friendly, one who is capable of working with all types of people. His ability to meet the public on its various levels and to build confidence probably are the specialists' strongest assets. Among the necessary basic skills are not only the ability to write and speak directly and clearly, but also a strong liking for such tasks. Ability to use graphics in print and other media also is useful.

PROFESSIONAL PREPARATION FOR THE DIRECTOR

The typical school administrator lacks the skills, knowledge and the know-how for a strong well-balanced public relations program. College graduate programs do not adequately prepare potential administrators in the area of public relations. Training is either completely lacking or is inadequate in quantity and quality. Professor L. S. Stiles, of Northwestern University, in a study of 131 institutions preparing candidates for the superintendency, discovered that only 60 offered any instruction in public relations. In almost all cases, the public relations instruction was presented by a professor of the college of education rather than one from the school of journalism. The report indicated that "four-fifths of the graduate students in educational administration have no opportunity to take either a major or a minor in the area of public information." There is need for greater cooperation between schools of education and schools of journalism; there is a great need to require future superintendents to have training in the area of public relations and information.

Mrs. Beatrice Gudridge, former associate director of NEA's press-radio-television division, recently admonished that when it comes to public relations ability, "too many educators are inept , in-grown and in a rut."

A typical school administrator in the field can develop his own public relations "self-help program." Since there is much written in the field of school-community relations he can obtain assistance and guidance from reading the literature. The many public relations workshops and seminars available on the local, state and national levels are especially helpful. Superintendents and public relations personnel can find many good ideas for eye-catching layouts to publish by requesting award-winning publications listed as winners of national contests. Outstanding publications, filmstrips, and messages can also be observed at the National School Public Relations Association display at the annual meeting of the American Association of School Administrators. School public relations publications and productions should occasionally be submitted to a panel of experts who render a critical analysis. Such panels are often found as part of state or national conventions.

Even the more talented school public relations experts learn from each other by exchanging materials.

Those responsible for the public relations program must constantly be alert to new ideas and techniques in order to develop new and creative approaches in the field. Robert Olds, School Management Inc., Columbus, Ohio, put it this way:

"A PR program, if it is to remain vigorous and purposeful, must have continuing sources of new ideas, adaptations and refinements. It also must keep abreast of changing conditions and developments. Most new ideas do not arrive in a dramatic creative flash. Rather, they emerge from a mental resorting, shuffling and modification of many elements. As I said earlier, the process has computerlike characteristics. But in many instances it is the bit of new information which sparks the process."

THE PUBLIC RELATIONS SPECIALIST DURING A CRISIS

The public relations specialist plays an important role during crisis periods such as a student walkout, a teacher strike, or a parent confrontation by serving as the chief spokesman for the board and superintendent. He is asked to answer questions presented by the news media representatives and by citizens. He shields the superintendent and board from the potential danger of making a poor or harmful statement. If the public relations man makes an error on a news release, it can always be explained that he wasn't fully informed. Such a reason can't be used by a board member or superintendent.

During periods of crisis the public relations person cannot take sides or argue an issue; his role is to answer questions and provide information. During emergencies, he needs to continue to contribute to the decision-making process. Because he works behind the scenes, and on a person-to-person basis, he is often able to present insights and objective opinions for management decisions.

CHAPTER III

A PUBLIC RELATIONS TOOL KIT

A PUBLIC RELATIONS TOOL KIT

As stated in the previous chapter, the typical school community is very diverse and is made up of many different groups or publics. Therefore, a variety of communication techniques must be used in an attempt to reach the many different constituents. Some citizens never read, but are avid users of radio and television and vice versa. Therefore school officials attempt to reach the citizens through a diverse set of communication tools and techniques.

PRINTED PUBLICATIONS

Printed school publications, although "one-way" media, are among the most widely used public relations instruments, because they provide a mass dissemination of school news. The effectiveness of school publications depends on proper layout, format, distribution and timing. Printed materials must have eye-appeal and contain current information. Additional guidelines for effective publications are presented in Chapter six (6).

The typical staff member is overwhelmed with demands on his time — papers to grade, lesson plans to prepare, school meetings to attend, community responsibilities: The average citizen has a similar problem; he is constantly bombarded with messages from the news media. People have to be discriminate in what they read. The following suggestions relate to effective printed materials:

> Publications designed for the staff and community must be brief. A voluminous publication, or even a one-page report which is single spaced or "wordy" in appearance, will not be read by most people.

> The layout should be conducive to quick reading — an underlined heading for each paragraph speeds up skimming a publication.

> The communication should be appealing in appearance.

> The story should be told truthfully.

> The communication should be balanced in content — there shouldn't be an overemphasis in one area, such as athletics.

The following publications are included in the tool kit of a school district attempting to promote an effective public relations program:

The School-Community Newsletter Those communities which have their own daily newspaper often have adequate school news coverage. Suburban communities adjacent to a large city, however, often lack adequate school news coverage in the daily newspaper because many school districts, political subdivisions and other organizations vie for space. Although the suburbs may have a weekly newspaper to complement the big-city editions, they seldom provide sufficient coverage. Rural districts face a similar problem. As a result, schools often publish their own newsletters on a monthly or bi-monthly basis. The publication assignment is usually given to a central office staff member; sometimes a teacher is given released time to edit the newsletter.

In order to compete with the mass media, the school-community newsletter must be well written and attractively designed. A publication which is too voluminous will not be read by many citizens. A brief two-to-six-page report will have better acceptance than an eight-or ten-page report. The newsletter which appears to be wordy or heavy with print will be cast aside by many. Therefore, there should be extensive use of "white space" and sizable margins. Photographs should be of good quality and should be used liberally. Often, help or advice on layout can be obtained from a member of the community who is employed in public relations work. The community newsletter should be printed by a professional printer. The school cannot afford to send out a publication which appears mediocre.

The newsletter should be mailed to every home in the school community. Allowing students to deliver them to their parents at the close of the school day is not an effective way of distribution. Many newsletters never reach home and adults without school-age children remain uninformed. The publication can be addressed in several ways:

A school secretary using an addressing machine

Contracting with a commercial mailing service

A citizens' mailing committee sponsored by a service organization such as the PTA Council; the addresses are written in longhand.

The latter method has two advantages:

(1) It saves the school money; (2) Citizens become involved in a positive school project.

In addition to the home mailing, additional copies should be sent to real estate offices, Chamber of Commerce, and the Welcome Wagon, where potential residents can read about the school system.

The contents of the newsletter must be of interest to the average citizen. NSPRA's publication — *Putting Words and Pictures About Schools Into Print* — states. . .

"As the regular, exclusive channel of communication between school and home, your community newsletter should tell what the system and its people (students, teachers, staff, and board) are doing and why. The newsletter should also be honest about what the system cannot do and why, and about such crises as drug abuse, student flare-ups, and discipline problems. This publication can give the citizenry a consistent monitoring on where tax dollars are going and what could be done with additional money."

A community newsletter should describe accomplishments as well as problems, successes as well as failures; it must report the "whole" school story.

The Staff Newsletter — The staff newsletter provides school employees with current school news. The publication should appear weekly, and a copy should be made available to each employee — professional and classified. It should have an eye-catching title and format. The newsletter must be brief (one or two pages) and written in a crisp and interesting style; white space should be used freely. Underlined paragraphs help break up the contents and permit easy skimming of the publication. It should be printed, not mimeographed.

The news carried in the newsletter should relate to the personnel for whom it was designed to reach. NSPRA's — *Putting Words and Pictures About Schools Into Print* — states:

> "Staff members in a school district usually want facts about developments that will affect them, information they can use in their work, and news about their colleagues. If teachers can go home at night and find out what happened in different parts of the world during the day, they surely ought to be able to expect some kind of news service about happenings in their own school system.

> "The publication should report about teachers with new ways to teach, administrators who have good ideas about administration, custodial workers who have found ways to cut costs, or school secretaries who know how to go out of the way to help parents, students, and teachers."

The staff newsletter should receive periodic evaluation. This can be accomplished through a questionnaire or an ad hoc evaluation committee can be appointed to interview staff members for evaluation.

An example of a staff newsletter is shown in Appendix B.

The School Board Report — A summary of the board of education meetings should be available to staff members and interested citizens the day after the meeting. Copies of the report should be placed in staff mailboxes as early in the day as possible in order to reduce a grape-vine version of what happened at the board session.

Some administrators are able to have board reports in the staff mailboxes before the employees arrive for work the morning after the board meeting. They use the following procedure: An administrator prepares the board summary as the meeting progresses. A central office secretary reports early the next day to type and duplicate the report; her quitting time is adjusted accordingly. A volunteer staff member is selected for each building who normally arrives early and who lives fairly close to the central office. This person, a secretary, teacher or custodian, picks up the copies on the way to work and delivers them to the building. The Board Report can be available to staff members as they arrive.

An example of a board report is shown in Appendix C.

Flash Report — Occasionally, a superintendent wishes to communicate an immediate message to his staff. News of a levy passage or approval of a salary adjustment might justify such a special effort. A unique letterhead, designed for a news release, allows the staff quick identification of a special message. (See Appendix D)

Report Card Stuffers — A message to parents can be placed on a "report card stuffer." The stuffer is a "mini report" limited to the size of the report card envelope. The message must be limited to a single topic and must be brief. Since the report is sent in the report card envelope, its chances of being received are improved over student-delivered reports. Topics that may be covered in report card stuffers include: "Enrollment Growths," "Costs of Education," "Sex Education in the Schools," "Science Curriculum." The pamphlet must be eye-catching and have a good layout.

Annual Report — The school annual report is one of the oldest forms of school reports. However, it is usually read by only the most dedicated of citizens. In order to increase readership, other techniques have been developed. Some superintendents produce an annual report in the form of a tabloid to be inserted in the daily newspaper. Other superintendents rely on a monthly or bi-monthly community newsletter to serve in lieu of the formal annual report. Colored slides or a movie can also be used to make the report. Such visuals can be shown at a regular board meeting and at community meetings.

USE OF RADIO AND TELEVISION

Many school districts which have radio and television media available in the community, fail to fully utilize the stations for school news dissemination. A certain echelon of every community can't or won't read the newspapers and rely entirely on radio and television for its source of news. Others in the community use radio and television, valuable one-way media, to supplement their newspaper reading.

Schools usually make use of radio and television for general school news, announcements of PTA meetings, concerts, plays and board of education meetings. Many schools, however, fail to use these facilities for "in-depth" programs of school topics or school needs. "In-depth" programs refer to detailed presentations on a single topic such as "How Our Schools Teach Reading." Such programs require talented leadership and time for planning and research. To assign the responsibility to an already overburdened staff member can result in mediocre broadcasts which could reflect negatively on the school. Therefore, if leadership, talent, and adequate time are not available, in-depth reports should be avoided.

Interviews and panels seem to be popular with radio and television managers and with viewing audiences; they can be aired with a minimum of pre-planning. Station personnel can be used to conduct the programs based on topics selected in advance by the school. School staff members are selected to fit the topic. The following topics were selected by one school for a once-a-week radio series:

Basic Adult Education
School Bus Service
Our Guidance Program
Humanities Program
School Discipline
New State Standards
The Work-Study Program
School Custodians At Work
Executive Teacher Program
Our Grading System
The PTA
Parent Conferences
Citizens' Committee
Materials Centers
The Head Start Program
Psychological Program
Remedial Reading
Individual Assistance Program

Teacher Salaries
School Financing
The Language Arts Program
Functions of the Board
The School Cafeteria
The ITA Program

The following guidelines apply to broadcasting:

Select interesting topics.

Speakers should be limited to staff members who speak reasonably well.

Publicize the programs — Use the student newspaper, the school menu news, the local newspaper.

Speakers should be positive in their approach; avoid negative attitudes.

Discussions should be informal; a presentation should never be read.

An increasing number of schools are purchasing closed-circuit television equipment for classroom use. The equipment can also be used by the public relations specialist. Staff-developed television tapes featuring teaching units, new teaching methods, or new curricula can also be used in the community relations program.

During a bond issue or levy campaign, key speakers can be video-taped making it possible for many groups to view the presentation at any time.

PARENT VISITS TO THE SCHOOLS

School officials have used many ways to bring parents into the schools. School visits provide an opportunity for parents to better understand the school program; they can also see firsthand some of the school needs. Many parents develop a "community pride" as a result of the school visitation.

Many parent visitations result during Open House programs sponsored by individual schools. Or, an invitation can be extended to visit classes in session during a designated week such as American Education Week. Teachers and principals may object to such a lengthy "open door" period because parents come and go and some students are distracted by the visits. Although some reduction in learning may occur, parent visits can result in better understanding and support of the school program. In the long run, students benefit. To protect the teacher from too much interruption, however, some basic ground rules for parent visits are necessary. For example, parents should not take preschool age youngsters into classrooms.

KAFFEE KLATSCH

Neighborhood "kaffee klatsches" can be used effectively for direct two-way communication with parents and citizens. The superintendent or building principal can make it known through the PTA or the school newsletter that he, representatives of his staff, and representatives of the board of education, are available for neighborhood meetings in which participants will discuss school subjects. As the kaffee klatsch comes to a close, the school representatives can invite those present to organize a similar meeting at a home or at the community library. The result can be a chain reaction of neighborhood meetings and an important breakthrough in "two-way" communications.

A PTA Council made up of representatives from each PTA unit can be an effective sponsor for a district-wide kaffee klatsch plan. One school PTA Council announced "March Is Know Your School Month" and organized neighborhood meetings throughout the community during this one-month period.

A school administrator may have difficulty starting such a project for lack of an invitation. He must then take the initiative and ask a PTA leader or a community leader to plan such a meeting. Hopefully, those who attend will receive sufficient benefit to be willing to organize additional sessions.

There are many variations of the kaffee klatsch plan. For example, parent meetings to discuss school programs or problems can be held at the local neighborhood school. Parents, however, seem to prefer the informality and warmth of a neighbor's living room to the structured school setting.

INFORMATION CENTERS

School "information centers" can be established in each elementary school attendance area. Each elementary principal is asked to identify 20 citizens who are well known, interested in schools, and are good communicators. Those selected will receive a letter from the Superintendent asking if they will serve as "information centers." In the letter they are assured that there will be no formal meetings and all communications will be conducted by mail. They are given "in-depth information" through a periodic newsletter and copies of the Board of Education Summary and special purpose reports are mailed to them. In return, these citizens are asked to disseminate as much school information as possible to neighbors and acquaintances, whether they meet them at the market or at social events. Information centers are an additional help in providing the community with maximum information.

AWARD CEREMONIES

Award ceremonies give recognition to deserving employees and add to the total public relations effort of the school district. Occasionally supporting community service organizations such as a Boosters Club or a Kiwanis Club can be recognized for their contributions to the school program. A "Certificate of Appreciation" can be presented by the board of education president to the president of the organization recognized. An excellent audience for such a ceremony is available during a student performance — a musical or athletic event. The board president, in addition to giving his appreciation, lists the many contributions made by the group recognized.

Certificates of recognition should also be awarded to employees who retire and to those who give long years of service. The latter group is usually recognized at five-year intervals. The certificates can be awarded by the board of education president during a regular meeting. In some school districts, the board of education, teachers' association and the noncertified association cooperate together to sponsor a staff recognition banquet during which the awards are presented.

THE HOME VISIT

The "home visit" made by a staff member to a student's home can provide an excellent home-school contact. Many schools involved in the Head Start Program have included home visits as a part of their planned program. Some Head Start Programs include a staff sociologist who works directly with the home. A few school districts have sociologists attached as a regular part of the school staff; home visits are a major function of such personnel. Because of the increased use of home visits, school staff members are becoming increasingly aware of the two-way public relations value of the visits.

Home visits are sometimes scheduled for kindergarten students during the first week of school in lieu of class attendance. Elementary students can be scheduled half-days during the first week of school to allow time for teachers to make home visits.

Carefully planned home visits can reap rich benefits for the teachers and the school; a poorly planned visit can create problems. Parents from low economic levels or from ethnic groups may feel uncomfortable in the presence of school representatives because they may dress or talk a little differently. Some parents might even suspect school personnel of snooping. Such reactions can be kept to a minimum if parents are prepared for the visit in advance and if the parents are shown the fullest respect and courtesy regardless of ethnic background or economic level.

The following guidelines may help in the planning of home visits:

A request to visit should be made, by telephone or letter, prior to the visit.

The visit should be kept brief — 20 minutes; 30 minutes as a maximum.

Avoid "talking down to people."

Avoid pedagogical terms; use simple words and sentences.

Do not dress in an ostentatious manner; make-up should be used with moderation.

Allow the first visit to get off to a positive start; avoid negative statements about the child.

Center most of the discussion about the child; questions about the home and family should be minimized to avoid suspicions of snooping.

Hazel Park, (Illinois) teachers have a home visitation program supported by both the school administration and the teachers' association. The following benefits are listed by Hazel Park officials as a result of the program:

— Parents will see a "real" teacher. No longer will they be misled by another person's interpretation.

— Staff will be exposed to the conditions that the child must live in — his physical and emotional environment.

— Staff will find out further why children are the way they are.

— Friendly channels of communication with the home will be open before "trouble" situations occur.

— The home and school can develop a partnership and understanding concerning the education of the child.

— Staff can observe the neighborhood conditions in light of the effect upon the child.

— Parents (and consequently the child) know they must really count if a professional person makes the effort to seek them out.

— Parents are more likely to respond favorably when staff members meet them on their own ground — their living room.

A REPORT TO THE COMMUNITY

Direct, face-to-face communication between the school staff and representative citizens should occur whenever possible. Some administrators facilitate such a meeting by sponsoring an annual "Report On Your School Banquet." Such an event can occur at either the building level (principal) or the district level (superintendent). As part of the program, the administrator and perhaps a board member present an overview of the year's progress, problems facing the school and future plans. Feedback can be obtained by concluding the program with an open discussion.

American Education Week presents an opportune time to schedule such a banquet. Often the community service clubs will sponsor the project, or it can be a project of the American Education Week Committee.

There are several ways to invite citizens to such an affair. All members of the community can be invited at a modest charge. Board members and influential citizens close to the school administrator must then encourage representatives of the community power structure to participate. An alternate approach is to ask each service club to select a quota to attend. The school administrator then works with service club officers to insure that influential citizens are invited.

OTHER PUBLIC RELATIONS TOOLS

School Programs — Printed "school programs" which are used for plays, musicals, and athletic events usually have space left over which can be used for public relations information. Influential citizens often attend such functions. Brief, interesting facts and statistics such as enrollment growth, staff increases, the amount spent per child for education, can be presented in the available space.

Speakers' Bureau — Many schools have organized speakers' bureaus composed of staff members and board of education members who are available to speak on various subjects. The topics need not be school related. An attractive brochure which indicates the speakers and their topics should be made available to community groups.

"TWO-WAY" VEHICLES

The following additional "two-way" public relations vehicles are especially strong in feedback potential:

46

The parent-teacher conference is a valuable two-way public relations vehicle. The teacher, however, must be encouraged to transmit feedback information to the administration. This return can be facilitated by asking each teacher to complete a written report describing parent comments. Additional feedback can be obtained by requesting the parent to complete a questionnaire at the conclusion of the conference. Space shall be provided for parent comments.

Informal community or neighborhood meetings held on special topics are effective. For example, if a school bond issue were defeated, meetings held in various sections of the community with a variety of groups or publics can be very revealing. Or, a public meeting on a controversial topics, such as "Drug Education" or "Religion in the Public Schools," can be very informative for citizens and allows school officials to better understand the community position and feeling about the subject.

Periodic meetings with special groups in the community can pay handsome public relations returns. Because local clergymen receive a great deal of community feedback about schools and because they are effective opinion molders, school officials should meet periodically with them. Some administrators schedule occasional meetings with the community barbers and beauty operators because schools are often discussed by their customers. One superintendent invited the groups listed above to lunch at a newly constructed school and to tour the new facilities.

If minority groups are present in the community, school officials should meet periodically with their leaders in order to have dialogue, allow for improved communications, and to provide feedback. Information from such meetings can often help school officials identify and solve problems before they cause real trouble.

Other two-way techniques such as the school questionnaire, community seminars, the citizens' advisory committee, and advisory groups are described in other chapters.

CHAPTER IV

PUBLIC RELATIONS
AND SCHOOL PERSONNEL:
Board of Education, Professional and Non-certified Personnel

PUBLIC RELATIONS
AND SCHOOL PERSONNEL:
Board of Education, Professional
and Non-certified Personnel

The previous chapters presented the basic ingredients needed for an effective public relations program, and some effective tools which can be used for the program. This chapter describes the important role played by those related to the school operation: board of education, principals, teachers and classified personnel.

THE BOARD OF EDUCATION

As a first step in planning an effective public relations program, the board of education should develop a public relations policy. The board members must also be public relations oriented in order to make the policy become effective and alive. The members must realize that the continued growth of the educational program will depend on community understanding and support of the school program and its goals. A board must, for example, provide the necessary funds and personnel to adequately operate the public relations program. An effective school-community program requires board members to give of their time and talent, since they will be expected to participate in many of the community-related programs.

The board must exemplify good public relations techniques to be in concert with the board-adopted policy on school-community relations. There must be continuous two-way communications between the board and the school staff and between the board and the school community. When the board acts on policies which affect staff members or portions of the community, the people affected should be given an opportunity to be heard before the board takes final action.

Each board member must realize that his own conduct in the community can have an important impact on the school's public relations program. He is asked many questions and hears much school-related information from citizens. It is important that he use discretion in answering questions and in channeling information, to the proper school official. For example, if a board member wants information, he should request it from the superintendent rather than from a staff member. Or, if a board member has a complaint related to a staff member or school program, it should be brought to the attention of the superintendent; the board member should not investigate or intervene on his own.

A superintendent is responsible for guiding his board toward the proper handling of staff and citizen communications. A suggested "Board-Superintendent Guideline" is presented in Appendix E.

The behavior of the board, as a group, is important. A secretive or autocratic board will cast a shadow of distrust upon the community. One which operates openly and is willing to examine all sides of a problem and makes decisions in open public meetings, will gain community confidence and trust.

Each board member must realize that he represents all of the people of the entire school district. He cannot represent any one geographic area or a particular interest group. His decisions as a board member must be based on what is best for the boys and girls of the entire school district.

The board must make a sincere attempt to solicit suggestions and opinions on the school operation from as many publics as possible. The reactions from the select group which attends board meetings and public hearings cannot be considered as representative of the entire community. The board must make overt attempts to obtain opinions from a more representative sampling of the community.

Keeping the Board Informed

A superintendent must determine how he can most effectively keep his board informed of what is happening in the school district; he must also decide how detailed the members want the information to be. A new superintendent should obtain some guidelines from his board at one of his first meetings with them. The beginning superintendent should also discuss how he can best obtain relevant information from his board members. In order to have maximum communication between the two parties, an atmosphere of mutual trust and respect must exist.

It's an important job to keep board members fully informed. They do not like to hear the news of a critical school problem or accident from a fellow citizen. Therefore, the superintendent must attempt to provide board members with maximum and, sometimes, instant news of school happenings. Board members can be informed through written memorandums, by telephone, and by calling a special board meeting.

Many superintendents provide their boards with regular weekly memorandums which describe the major events of the week and the activities in which the superintendent and his staff have been involved. Rather than use the postal service for delivery, which results in a delay of a day or two, many superintendents send the reports to board members by a school messenger. The memorandum should not be wordy; it should be concise and free of educational jargon.

The weekly memorandum may be supplemented with special memos as the needs arise. If an especially critical event occurs, such as a negotiations problem or if a teacher is struck by a student, the superintendent will need to immediately telephone each board member. At certain critical times, the board members need to convene for a personal report from the superintendent. Such a meeting would be justified, for example, on the evening of a threatened strike so the board could be apprised of the differences existing between the negotiating teams. The most effective communications result from the person-to-person dialogue which is possible in such meetings.

Copies of important press releases should first be sent to the board, before they are released. Board members do not like to read or hear information from the news media with no previous knowledge.

Effective Board Meeting

The board agenda should be prepared and in the hands of board members several days prior to the official board meeting. If a member is strongly opposed to an agenda topic or to the wording or an item, time is available for revisions.

After board changes, if there are any, representatives of the news media should receive copies. This should be done as soon as possible following Board approval of the agenda. The media people, too, like to review the agenda prior to the board meeting.

Board meetings should be held in a large enough room to handle the normal turnout of citizens. Seating should be adequate, ventilation and temperature comfortable, the room should be esthetically pleasant. An auxiliary room or auditorium should always be ready as a standby, should an overflow crowd appear. If the board room overflows and the board refuses to move to a larger facility, resentment toward the board will occur.

A welcoming brochure should be available for those who attend the board sessions which includes a brief biographical sketch of each board member, explains how the board meeting proceeds and outlines how citizens in attendance can participate in the board meeting proceedings.

A name plate should appear before each individual who is seated at the board table. The lettering should be large enough to be visible in the back of the room. If citizens have difficulty hearing at board sessions, microphones should be installed.

Many boards of education reserve a table and chairs for members of the news media. A plate similar to a name plate which states "Reserved for the News Media" should be stationed on the table. A similar table should be reserved for representatives of the teachers' association and a name plate, "Reserved for the Teachers Association," placed on the table.

Executive sessions should be avoided during, before or after a regularly scheduled board meeting. Executive sessions held during the meeting are especially resented for the meeting is interrupted and there is a boring lag for those in attendance. Executive sessions at any time result in distrust and suspicion toward board members. On rare occasions, however, they are needed.

Each citizen who addresses the board should be required to give his name and address. This procedure identifies him for school officials and for members of the news media. It also may temper the remarks of the visitor.

Civic organizations should be encouraged to appoint a school representative to attend board meetings and to report school news back to the membership. The board president should ask each such representative in attendance to stand, give his name and the name of his organization. Such identification provides recognition for both the individual and the organization.

Attendance at board meetings can be increased by announcing the meeting dates in the news media available to the board: newspapers, radio, television, school-community newsletters. Interest can also be spurred if the superintendent or board president is interviewed on radio or television the afternoon prior to the board meeting. At the interview the school official can outline or review the major topics to be covered in the evening meeting.

Educational Topic

An educational topic related to some aspect of the school program should be included on the board agenda at least once a month. Such a topic allows the board to become involved in other areas than the routine policy-making and operation of the school district. The board and administration determine a series of topics which they believe board members and citizens should know more about. One such topic is selected for each board meeting. Staff members are selected to develop the topic as an educational program. This allows teachers and administrators to explain programs in which they are involved and provides recognition and exposure for them. Typical subjects chosen for educational topics might include: The Changing High School; School Discipline; School Vandalism; Teaching Controversial Subjects; Students' Rights.

The educational topic information can be further disseminated in the school community in the following manner: local newspaper, student newspaper (through a press conference with superintendent);

school-community newsletter, elementary level newsletters; talks to civic groups and P. T. A.'s; local radio show.

The educational topic allows school officials to use the board meeting as a platform to initiate an informational program on important school concepts which need to be explained to the community. Other media available to the school should then be used to further amplify the message to a maximum degree.

A caution: The program should be limited in time — perhaps to 30 minutes. The participants should be required to conduct a "dry run" prior to the board meeting. The practice session will allow participants to polish up the presentations and estimate the time required. Educators, because of their enthusiasm for a topic, have a natural tendency to exceed time allotments. Such abuse can reduce board enthusiasm toward the educational topic.

Other Techniques Used to Improve Board-Community Relations

Before important board decision are made, community input (opinions and concerns) must be considered and weighed. Such input can be obtained in several ways. A committee of citizens and educators can study the problem and provide the board with its findings. Or, a public hearing on the subject can be held.

A "board team" should periodically make itself available at various locations in the community for an informal discussion on public education. An open invitation should be extended to all citizens to attend. A neutral setting, such as a community library, provides an excellent location for such a meeting. The board team usually includes the board president, the superintendent, a secondary principal, an elementary principal and a classroom teacher. Such sessions provide an excellent source of community feedback for the board of education and administration to consider.

The board president and superintendent can be available 30 minutes prior to each board meeting to provide time for citizens who wish to have an individual, private conference. Some citizens are too modest to present problems at a formal board meeting. Such people have an opportunity of arriving early for a private conference.

Communications between the board and citizens can be enhanced through a program entitled "Breakfast With the Board." Such breakfasts scheduled on Saturday mornings can be sponsored by P.T.A. units and are usually located at an elementary site. Participants are largely from the school's attendance area. Representatives of the board of education, the superintendent, the building principal and several classroom teachers usually attend. Following breakfast, an open discussion is held with those in attendance.

THE BUILDING PRINCIPAL

The building principal can be very effective in school-community work because he is close to the students, parents and the neighborhood. As a result, many districts are decentralizing much of their public relations work to the building level.

Principals are not always receptive to public relations involvement. Many are already overburdened and overextended with the operation of their respective schools. The principal, however, who realizes that community support is necessary in order to have continued growth in the educational program, is quick to realize the importance of effective school-community relations and will give priority to work in this area.

The building principal must apply the basic principles of public relations in his school operation, as presented in Chapter one:

— He must have an effective educational program; the challenged child will bring home positive reports of his school.

— He must be "visible" to his constituents — students, staff and citizens.

— He must have a balance in his communications efforts — written publications vs. person-to-person contacts.

— He must show respect and courtesy to his best school supporters as well as to his most vocal critics.

The Principal and Staff Morale

The building principal determines the public relations tone for his building and community by the way he relates to students, staff and citizens. The principal who is strong in human relations will have good communications with teachers, students and adults. His attitude, his enthusiasm, his way of greeting staff members, students and adults will reflect in the climate of school and the esprit de corps which exists among the staff, students and citizens. His leadership will also reflect in student behavior, and student achievement, P.T.A. attendance and citizens support at the polls.

The building principal must be able to stimulate his staff to maximum production; he must spur them to continued in-service work. He must give recognition to those who show outstanding performance. Conflicts and confrontations are more numerous today; these can divide and polarize a faculty. The principal with human relations skills can reduce staff friction and develop harmonious staff working relations.

Working With Staff

Faculty meetings should be held only when the need arises. Staff information or directions should be given in memos whenever possible. Teachers' meetings which include inane topics or which are too lengthy are considered as an abuse of teachers' time; staff resentment toward the administrator occurs. As a result, teachers have negotiated clauses into their contract agreements which require the building principal to distribute an agenda prior to staff meetings, prohibit reading materials to teachers and include time limits for the meetings. Such practices should be followed anyhow.

Principals should allow staff input in preparing the agenda. Some time should be allowed during the meeting for staff discussion and input.

The building principal can help keep his staff informed by developing a teachers' handbook which contains the basic information and policies which all teachers should know. The public-relations conscious principal will occasionally include a public-relations suggestion or idea in his staff newsletter. He will provide in-service programs to help staff members sharpen their skills in special areas as parent conferences and field trips.

Developing News Stories

A principal must be alert to potential news stories. The following newsgathering techniques for building principals are suggested for Highland Park, Illinois administrators:

PRINCIPAL'S GUIDE TO SCHOOL NEWS REPORTING

— Enlist the aid of teachers and ask them to submit stories about their classroom activities.

— Enlist the aid of students — even to the extent of having a youngster write the news from a particular grade or class. If this is done, sign their names, and by-line credit will be given.

— Visit classrooms to see what activities and projects are under way. Very often a teacher may not recognize that a particular event or activity is newsworthy.

— Collect school news through class projects. Each week or month a different class can cover the school.

— Ask the school secretary and custodian. Both are usually good sources of information about human interest stories.

— Read what other schools have printed in the newspaper and school district publications.

What is good school news? Good school news is partially what the public wants to read and partially the phases of education school officials would like them to know about. Belmont Farley, former Director of Press and Radio, National Education Association, suggests the following list of subjects of what people want to know about their schools. Included are suggestions on what makes news in each category.

Pupil Progress And Achievement
Success stories of students and graduates. Keep a watch over the students' outside activities — often they are related to, or dependent on school work, awards, honor rolls (if they are not too long), graduations, contests, or festivals.

Methods Of Instruction
Special projects carried out by a class such as puppet shows, choral reading.

Any project that is unusual, interesting, or carried out in a different way.

Results of new methods of instruction in comparison with the old way. This is particularly good if a marked response is found to the new method, or if there is something concrete to show in student learning.

Health Of Pupils
Specific health projects carried out by a class; for instance, a class study of a health problem, or of T.B. near Christmas seal time. The lower elementary grades may even produce something interesting in the use and study of toothbrushes.

Courses Of Study
Much of this subject may be covered by directors, but feature angles usually can originate in the classroom. Examples: how a subject is taught and individual student's reactions.

Value Of Education
Indicate through achievements, results, and application. How a student mastered a particular hobby, or obtained a promising job through school training.

Discipline And Behavior
Good deeds.
Patriotic displays.
Good manners projects.

Teachers And Officers
Professional activities of teachers and administrators; conference and convention attention, election or appointment to a professional office, professional honor award, book or article publication, special recognition of any kind of professional work or community activity. Teachers' meetings or workshops.

Attendance
Attendance records of unusual length, or perfect attendance under unusual circumstances.
Attendance contests.

School Buildings
Feature angles on unusual use of classrooms or equipment. Newer buildings remain in the spotlight for some time. New innovations in the older buildings often lend themselves to several good stories.

Extracurricular Activities
Student plays, programs, intramural sports, clubs.

Working With Students

A principal must use techniques to develop a positive spirit among the students of his building. He needs to spend time with them — to talk, to listen, to rap. Many principals in small and medium-sized buildings know each student by name — an excellent step toward developing good rapport.

Ways must be developed to give students recognition. Award Days are sponsored; certificates are presented to students who excel in scholarship and in student activities. Students who serve on the school safety patrol can be honored with a visit to a professional baseball game. A student who has been a chronic behavior problem and shows improvement should be personally complimented by the principal.

One principal asked his teachers to send him one child a week who had accomplished something outstanding such as art work, a test score, or an improved homework assignment. The principal discussed the accomplishment with the pupil and then placed the product in a place of honor on the school bulletin board or showcase. A second-grade student once brought the principal a perfect spelling paper, listened carefully to how it would be displayed on the bulletin board, and softly said, "Wow!"

Another principal sponsored a "Student of the Month Contest." Each room selected a student of the month based on criteria established by principal and the staff. From this group, each month a "School Citizen of the Month" was chosen to represent the entire school. The "School Citizen" was selected by a committee composed of representatives from the administration, faculty, bus drivers, custodians, secretaries and student council. The monthly school winner had his or her photograph placed on the school bulletin board with a caption, "School Citizen of the Month." The monthly winners and their parents were also honored at the end of the year with a banquet attended by community leaders.

The Principal and His Community

The building principal must know his community — how it is organized, its values and mores, its power structure. In order to be knowledgeable in these areas, the administrator must spend time in his community; he must have opportunities to meet people. Principals who live in their attendance area have an advantage because they can better get to know the community make-up.

There are other ways to become familiar with a community. One principal solicited the help of his PTA president to better know her attendance area. The two of them, as a team visited homes at random in the community to become acquainted with parents and to obtain feedback information.

All members of the school staff should be encouraged to become active in civic organizations. Such participation allows them to be introduced to other citizens and community leaders; it also helps them to broaden their interests into areas other than public relations.

The school administrator needs to do additional work in areas of his community which are nonsupportive of the school. Such areas can be identified by reviewing precinct voting records on school issues. A principal may also be able to identify an area of his community where citizens seldom participate in school projects or programs. The principal can motivate citizens' interest and participation in such apathetic areas in several ways:

1. He can, personally, invite citizens in such areas to serve on school committees.

2. Representatives of the area can be personally invited by the principal for a coffee hour or for lunch — in order to obtain citizen opinions or appraisals of the school operation.

3. The principal and staff members can conduct home visits in the area.

4. Representatives of the area can be employed as teachers, paraprofessionals, or cafeteria employees. By working in the school, the employee will better understand the school operation and return to communicate school information to the community.

Other techniques used by principals to develop improved school-community relations include:

Weekly Newsletter to Parents — Many elementary principals prepare weekly mimeographed newsletters for parents and send them home with the students. Often included is the next week's school lunch menu to stimulate parent interest in the publication. Secondary principals who prepare parent newsletters find it best to mail them to the parents. Students in grades 7 - 12 cannot be relied upon for delivery of school literature to the homes. The news items in a principal's parent newsletter are largely related to the particular building. A limited amount of information pertaining to the entire school district and to community events is also included. (An example of a parent newsletter is shown in Appendix F.)

Weekly Newsletter for Staff — Staff members must be well informed if they are to work effectively in the classroom and if they are to be effective in the school's public relations program. In addition to the staff newsletter prepared by the superintendent, many principals publish their own weekly staff newsletter for those in their own buildings.

Citizen Volunteers — The principal should encourage maximum use of volunteers for his building. He must first, however, prepare his staff to use this potential help; staff members must want such assistance; volunteers cannot be forced upon teachers. Most principals begin a volunteer program on a low key. If one or two teachers are willing to use volunteers, other staff members soon see the advantages of additional help and make requests for additional volunteers.

Volunteers serve effectively in the classroom, cafeteria, library, playground, duplicating room. The volunteers should be given in-service training for their assignments before being placed on the job. As a result of working in schools, volunteers will have a better understanding of the school operation and will serve as effective communicators when they return to the community.

Coffee Hours — Principals have found informal coffee hours, held weekly for citizens of their community, to be very effective in improving parent communications. If such coffee hours, however, are merely announced through the local newspaper or radio, attendance is likely to be minimal or zero. Citizens response is improved if a building administrator personally invites a sampling of parents by telephone. At such meetings, the principal usually allows open discussions on parent concerns and questions. Coffee hours provide excellent two-way communications; citizens' misunderstandings and misinformation can be reduced.

Visual Aids and the School Story — A collection of slides or a movie of the school in action or of a new curriculum program are valuable for PTA programs, coffee hours and many other school programs. The more students involved in the pictures, the more effective the public relations tool will be.

Operate an Effective School Office — The principal's secretary should be warm, gracious and courteous. Residents wishing to visit the principal should have a pleasant waiting area — comfortable chairs, current reading materials, decor in good taste. The principal should be prompt for appointments; greet visitors in a friendly manner. Correspondence should be answered promptly.

A Well-Kept School — When visitors approach a school, their first impressions are important: the appearance of the school grounds, walkways, doorways. The principal must insist that his building is maintained neat and tidy. Shrubbery must be trimmed, debris removed, windows kept clean. The hallways must be clean; bulletin boards and show cases should appear current, colorful and reflect the school program. At the main entrance(s) to the school, signs should indicate the direction of key facilities: principal's office, cafeteria, gymnasium, primary grades, upper grades. The first impressions are lasting impressions, and are often used to judge the entire school operation.

The role of the building principal and the PTA and his role with various advisory groups are presented in Chapter ten.

The building principal must be able to identify the influential citizens of his community and seek their cooperation and support. In Chapter fourteen, the community and its power structure are discussed.

The building principal must continuously work on improving his public relations skills. This can be accomplished by keeping abreast of the literature and by occasionally attending public relations seminars. Because effective communications rely so much on writing and speaking skills, the administrator needs to constantly work on refining his competence in these areas. Human relations skills are very important to today's school administrator; help in this area also needs to be sought.

THE SCHOOL STAFF — PROFESSIONAL AND NONCERTIFICATED

The school staff (teachers, custodians, secretaries, bus drivers) play important roles in the school public relations program.

The "esprit de corps" or feelings of the school staff are enhanced by a good internal communications program which provides the staff with a maximum of information; with information as soon as it becomes available and before it reaches the news media. A staff with a good spirit and attitude is important and more influential than the total efforts of the formal school public relations program — including its publications and the many community speeches. The staff's feelings about their schools permeates the entire community. For example, their feelings carry over to the students who in turn carry them home to their parents. Their feelings carry over to friends and acquaintances who they meet outside of school. The staff which believes they are working for a good and just school will carry these feelings to all they meet; a most positive public relations effect will result.

Those members of the community who have a school-related question and who know a school employee, will seek the answer from this friend; he will also expect the friend to know the answer and will believe the reply without question. Therefore, school officials must do all they can to keep employees fully informed. Staff members want to know what is going on in the schools. They, like board members, don't want to hear school news from a neighbor. Whenever possible, they should receive news through school channels before it is released to the community. A new edition of the school-community newsletter, for example, should be placed in each staff mailbox before it is mailed to the community.

The staff member usually receives school information through:

Newsletters and bulletins prepared by the superintendent and principal.

Meetings of the staff or of small groups of the staff to receive information on special topics.

It is also important to allow staff input on the operation of the school, the school program and on decisions which affect employees.

The superintendent's staff newsletter can be written occasionally in the form of a questionnaire to allow employees to evaluate the school's communications program and to invite suggestions for improving the informational efforts.

The school principal and superintendent should occasionally have lunch with staff members. Administrators should occasionally visit with staff members in the teachers' lounge or lunch room. The informal atmosphere in these locations provides an opportunity for teachers and administrators to better relate to one another.

On occasions, the superintendent and building principal should tour the building as a team, visiting teachers and noncertificated personnel as time allows. If a staff member makes a request for assistance or for information, the request should never go unfulfilled. Either the request should be realized, or the reason why it couldn't should be returned.

The Staff in the Community

Staff members play an important public relations role when they participate in community activities and while involved in social contacts in the community. The results of such interaction can be either positive or negative for the school, depending on the judgment and intent of the school employee involved. Members of the community have "ready ears" in the presence of school personnel because they know school people carry a reservoir of school news. Whenever information about students, school staff members, or school policy is revealed to a friend at a bridge party or supermarket, it is very likely to be amplified in the community. It is sometimes tempting for the school employee to provide "newsy items" in discussions since he then becomes the center of attraction. But, when indiscreet information is revealed, the boys and girls and the school suffer. In a positive vein, school personnel can transmit much valuable and accurate information to the community in such personal contacts. Many times rumors can be squelched by an alert school representative.

Staff Recognition

Staff members who do outstanding work should receive recognition and praise whenever possible. An administrator can indicate such appreciation verbally or in the form of a note. The following letter was written by a principal to a noncertified staff member at the conclusion of a successful parent program:

"Your help in setting up and cleaning up for our P.T.A. family potluck was tremendously appreciated. The fact that you came in early to help out is typical of the conscientious way you do your job every day.

"I was very pleased that your family was able to attend and share part of the evening with us.

"You have been a tremendous addition to our staff and we've all been very pleased with your fine work and excellent attitude."

The person or group who did outstanding work can also be recognized through a news article released concerning the assignment. Photographs add to such a release. Exceptional individual work or an effective department effort can be featured in the staff newsletter or in the school-community publication. For example, the food service program or the science department can be presented in such bulletins. The board of education can provide recognition through an educational topic presented at each board session.

The use of staff advisory committees is explained in Chapter Ten.

THE CLASSROOM TEACHER

The board of education and school administrators can make the most significant contribution to the school public relations program by recruiting the best possible teachers for classroom assignments. Excellent teachers make possible an effective educational program which results in well taught students — the best public relations ambassadors a school can have.

All applicants for teaching positions should receive courteous treatment. Those who are hired will appreciate and remember their first contacts with school officials. Those who are not employed will reflect on their treatment while employed in another district. Each letter of inquiry or application should be answered by a school official. Those who are employed should receive a letter of welcome from the principal and superintendent. They should also immediately receive a copy of the staff handbook; literature which describes the school district and community; recent editions of the staff newsletter, board reports and school-community newsletter. The new staff member should be introduced to his superintendent, principal, department chairman and other supervisory personnel, before he or she begins work. Some principals assign a "buddy teacher" to help the new staff member. The orientation program for new staff personnel should provide as much information as possible. After school has been underway for several weeks, new employees should be asked to evaluate the orientation program. From the feedback, administration should obtain information to improve future orientation programs.

Teachers and News Stories

Staff members can make significant public relations contributions by suggesting potential news stories and news photos to the building reporter, who, in turn, will channel the information to the district's public relations coordinator.

The classroom teacher, because of the status of his position, is potential news. Anything he does which is unusual, good or bad, can result in a story. Depending on the incident, this can be a positive or negative influence on the school image.

School officials should also publicize staff activities which occur outside of the school program. The story should be told of school personnel who are active in community affairs in order to improve the community's image of the professional educator.

Teachers and Effective Public Relations

The community expects the classroom teacher to maintain adequate discipline in the classroom. A poorly disciplined class reflects negatively upon the entire staff and the school. Old-fashioned disciplinary techniques which are psychologically unsound, and which irritate parents include: (1) group punishment, (2) forced apologies before a class, (3) ridicule.

Teachers can improve the classroom atmosphere by maintaining bright cheerful surroundings. Colorful student art can be displayed, bulletin boards should be current, plants add color and serve for science demonstrations. The teacher who involves students in maintaining an attractive classroom helps instill a feeling of pride in each of them.

Classroom teachers willing to sponsor student activity programs before school, after school or during the noon hour help students and help improve the school's image. Elementary students, for example, enjoy learning specialized skills such as photography, chess, intramural sports. Parents are very appreciative of teachers who give of their time to develop such specialized skills.

Some teachers prepare a welcome letter for each student prior to the opening of school. Information such as the time to report and what to bring for the first day of school is included.

Community Resources

Teachers can relate to the community by making effective use of field trips and by inviting citizens to the classroom who can contribute to a particular learning unit. Many schools provide teachers with brochures which list suggested field trips and recommend citizens' talent. Use of such community resources enhance the curriculum; a secondary benefit is an opportunity for citizens to make positive contributions to the school program, "to get involved." Community participation also allows the school to interpret its program, curriculum and staff to the community.

69

Teachers and the Telephone

Teachers in some districts use the telephone to improve home-school relations. Usually, when parents receive a school call it indicates trouble for their child. To remove this stigma, some teachers make "good news calls" to compliment parents about their children. In some schools, the teachers' associations have sponsored such a project and asked each teacher to make at least one "good news call" a week. In this way, thousands of positive messages are relayed to the community each year. One school went so far as to establish special lines and carrells to give teachers privacy for the calls.

Teachers also make use of the telephone for parent conferences. Because of increased busing and because of school consolidations, it is more difficult for parents to travel the distance to school to confer with the teachers. Although telephone calls are not as satisfactory as face-to-face meetings, it is better than none at all. The following suggestions are recommended by NSPRA to make telephone conferences more effective:

Inform parents in advance, by letter, when you plan to call. Ask them to suggest an alternate time, if your choice is not convenient. State briefly what you want to talk about, and suggest some questions they may want to ask. Let the youngster know you're going to make the phone call. Ask him what he would like you to discuss with his parents.

When you make the call, avoid starting off with a long speech. You want to learn as well as to inform, so ask questions that call for more than "yes" or "no" answers.

Remember that the parent on the other end of the line cannot see your facial expressions, so he is supersensitive to the sound of your voice. If you sound gruff or critical, your call may do more harm than good.

End the call with several action suggestions — things parents can do on the home front. Close on a positive, optimistic note. Try to work out a convenient time for a face-to-face meeting.

Make notes during the conversation. You may get information about the child that you can use later. Or, the parent may ask questions you cannot answer immediately. Write the questions down and promise to write or call later.

A Public Relations Idea

An interesting student contest which has educational as well as a public relations value is entitled "Citizen of the Month." Based on a set of criteria, one student is selected at the close of each month. The recipient has his picture taken with the school camera. Two prints are made. One photo is placed in a prominent place on the room bulletin board. The students's parents receive the second photo with a personal note to the parents, written by the teacher.

Developing a Positive Self-Image

Students are influenced by each word, movement or expression which the teacher shares with her students. A youngster with a positive self-image will be an asset to the school and to the school community relations program. The following teacher techniques used to help students develop a positive self-image were described by Mr. Edward Kubany in the September, 1972 edition of *Teacher:*

Giving Praise

That's really nice.
Thank you very much.
Wow!
That's great.
I like the way you're working.
Keep up the good work.
Everyone's working so hard.
That's quite an improvement.

Giving Attention

Smile, give a pat or nod your head in approval.
Say, "I see you really understand."
Have others compliment him.
Call on him in class when you are sure he can give a good answer.

Remark to the class, "Johnny is working harder."
Complimentary note to parent.
Complimentary phone call to parent.
Read a story to him.

Privileges

Dismiss him a few seconds early; or, let him be first in the row to leave.
Let his row go first.
Excuse him from doing homework — announce this aloud.
Have him be lavatory supervisor.
Give him a ride home.
Invite him to an out-of-school special activity.
Have him be a line leader.
Give him free time; a few minutes is adequate.
Request his help as a personal favor.
Have him get his coat first.
Have him act as "teacher" for a discussion game.
Seating in desirable spots.
Extra lavatory break
Director of rhythm band.
Allowing to tutor another child.
"Teacher aid" for the day.
Erase board.
Decorate bulletin board.
Establish a game corner.

Giving Tasks

Use him to demonstrate a correct method.
Have him feed pets in the room.
Have him pass out books, papers, etc.
Dust the erasers.
Make him class monitor.
Have him help a handicapped child in or out of the school.
Clean blackboard trays of chalk dust.
Appoint him tutor to a needy classmate or younger child.

Token Reinforcers

A star
A sticker

A checkmark
VG (very good), E (excellent)
Post his work on a prominent bulletin board.
Post his name on the board.

THE SUBSTITUTE TEACHER

Substitute teachers can enhance public relations or they can be detrimental to public relations; much depends on the reception and treatment they receive from the students and teachers of the buildings they serve. A substitute teacher usually serves several school districts in a particular geographic area. The substitute teacher develops opinions of each school or school district which he serves — the warmth, courtesy, friendliness and quality of the staff and students. Many of them freely disseminate their subjective evaluations and opinions in the community.

The following admonishment, written by a California teacher, emphasizes the importance of courteous treatment for the substitute teacher:

"Some schools I eagerly look forward to visiting. Some are happy, kind, and warm. Others are cold and cruel. No matter how busy a principal or teacher is, it does not take any time or effort to nod a 'good morning.'

"To be entirely ignored in the lunchroom is thoughtless, too. Being left out is at its worst there. A solitary lunch is not so pleasant as a companionable one. Hearing happy conversations going on without one word directed in your direction has its bad moments. I hope regular teachers reading this will remember."

The building principal must insist that each teacher have the next day's lesson plans prepared before leaving the building at the close of the day. In case of teacher absence, the substitute teacher will then have directions. The principal must also continuously emphasize the importance of being courteous and respectful to the substitute teachers. This emphasis should extend to students and to the staff. He, himself, will set the example by his own relationship or behavior toward the substitute.

THE NONCERTIFIED STAFF

The noncertified employees (secretaries, custodians, bus drivers, cafeteria employees, maintenance staff) are the most neglected personnel in school public relations.

Too often the administrator forgets about the noncertified staff and their part in the public relations program — those who take his phone calls, greet visitors and play host to the public. The administrator needs to be reminded that the citizens' first impression of the school often results from the efforts of the nonteaching staff. Such first impressions as the appearance of the building and grounds, the way a visitor is greeted by the secretary or custodian are important and lasting.

The noncertificated staff members are especially valuable in school-community relations because they are in contact with segments of the community which are often not accessible to members of the professional staff. These segments seek school information from the nonteaching group. These employees carry prestige in the eyes of their friends because they are employed by the board of education. The school information which these employees furnish is accepted without questions. Therefore, it is most important for school officials to keep the noncertified employees fully informed and as supportive members of the school team.

CHAPTER V

**PUBLIC RELATIONS:
PARENTS AND STUDENTS**

PUBLIC RELATIONS:
PARENTS AND STUDENTS

COMMUNICATIONS WITH PARENTS

The school has an effect or influence on what many parents value the most: their child and their pocketbook. And, they want to know about both of their treasures. They want to know how their child is being taught, what he is taught, and how successfully he is being taught. They want to know how their school dollar is being spent and how effectively it is being spent. To answer such vital parent questions, school officials have developed many tools of communication which are suggested in several chapters of this book.

A child's attitudes, values, and habits are formed as the result of interactions with many individuals: parents, teachers, other adults and other children who associate with the child. The greatest over-all influence on the youngster, however, is the parent. Most of a person's attitudes, habits and values are formed while in the care of parents, before the child reaches school age. The teacher, however, also has a very pronounced influence on the development of a student. If the two most influential adults — the parent and the teacher — can cooperate to influence the child in a positive manner, much can be accomplished. If, however, they are at odds, their potential influence will be greatly reduced.

Parent School Visits

Parents will become better acquainted with the school program if they feel free to occasionally visit the schools. They will also become more understanding and supportive. Many schools maintain an open-door policy and encourage parents to visit at any time. Others sponsor special events to encourage parent visitation: open house, parent conferences, coffee hours. Some teachers use the culmination of a teaching unit as an opportunity to invite parents. At this time students present reports or display projects. A study of Japan, for example, can be culminated with a Japanese luncheon to which parents are invited. It is an excellent time to expose parents to classroom activities and accomplishments.

Advice for Parents

School officials in many districts provide preschool parents with advice, suggestions and help in rearing their children prior to their arrival at school. Parents are encouraged to provide their children with meaningful educational experiences, and they are advised on how to develop a home setting conducive to learning.

Some building principals occasionally send parents a bulletin which suggests ways parents can provide specific educational activities or experiences. Typical of such suggestions are:

Take your child to the library once a week.

Read to your child each day.

Encourage your child to talk, for he needs to express himself.

Provide suitable books, supplies, and games.

Visit your community — parks, museums, airports, industries.

An elementary school in San Bernardino, California, distributed brochures which listed educational activities for families. A different publication was provided for each age group. For example, under the heading, "Are You Helping Your 8 or 9 Year Old Grow as a Person This Summer?" appeared:

"Have you decided WITH him:

— what he should do in an emergency

— where he can play safely

— some excursions the family may enjoy together

— when his friends may visit?"

A Plymouth, Connecticut, school published a mimeographed letter, "The Play Way to Reading," which encouraged parents to play learning games with their children.

Many school buildings are plagued with chronic vandalism. Parents can help reduce such destruction. An elementary principal sent the following letter to each parent in his attendance area:

"Dear Neighbor:

"During the summer months you may observe a great deal of activity on the school property.

"Children are welcome to use the playground, ball fields, etc. However, we do not want any vandalism, nor children playing in any area that bothers the neighbors. Also, we would prefer that ball games not be played in the front yard.

"If you observe any incidents that you feel would cause damage to property, please report the information to the school (_____) or to the Police (_____).

"Thank you for your help and cooperation."

Using Citizen Talent

The typical community includes citizens with many talents. Most school officials have barely begun to tap this valuable reservoir of highly skilled persons. Such adults should be identified and those who are willing to share talents with the school should be invited to do so. In one school, a parent skilled as a bricklayer brought brick and mortar to the school to demonstrate construction of a brick wall. In the same school, a barber demonstrated how to cut hair; a ballet dancer, the

79

COMMUNITY TALENT

We are convinced that our school district has many untapped physical and human resources that could enrich the school program. There are many talented individuals in a variety of fields — science, commerce, industry, trades, film, dance, fine arts — who could add a great deal to the lives of many young people.

Please help us identify those people in our communities who might be willing to devote two or three days each year to volunteering as resource people in our schools.

Would you (or your neighbor, friend, business associate) be willing to discuss or demonstrate occupational skills, hobbies, or travel experiences?

If you, or anyone you know, might be willing to be "one of us" please check the proper category and return the tear sheet to your school or to

_____ .

| (Name) | (Address) | (Phone) |

Occupational Skills

____ engineering
____ law
____ medicine
____ tool and die
____ finance
____ landscaping
____ aviation
____ journalism
____ architecture
____ art, music, theatre
____ construction
____ other

Hobbies

____ culinary arts
____ dramatics, music
____ sewing, knitting
____ puppets, dolls
____ ceramics
____ leather crafts
____ woodworking
____ model trains, cars
____ aquariums, birds
____ yoga, karate
____ dancing
____ nature studies
____ sports
____ other

Travels

____ U. S.
____ Europe
____ Asia
____ Africa
____ S. America
____ other

Can you give us the name of anyone in the school community whom we should contact about special skills or interests?

| (Name) | (Address) | (Phone) |

Figure 3 — Instrument to Identify Community Talent

ballet; a photographer, development of prints. Those citizens who have skills which can be used by the schools must be sought out. One building principal used the instrument shown in Figure 3 to identify potential parent talent; it was sent home with each child.

Other Citizen Roles

Parent-teacher conferences are one of the best vehicles available to improve parent-staff communications.

Parent participation in the school operation has been greatly increased through the utilization of volunteers. Volunteers, as a result of their work, can better understand the school operation and school problems, and they communicate this understanding when they return to their home community.

Parents Squeezed Out

Parents have become squeezed out of many school activities. This has occurred because of the following recent trends:

Busing of students into distant and strange communities makes it difficult for parents to be informed and involved in the school operation.

The militancy of staff members in some districts has alienated citizens. Strike threats, militant statements and walkouts have reduced community support for education.

Since school consolidations have created large districts; parents feel more removed from the school operation.

To be effective, the school needs the support, cooperation and interest of the parents. This is true whether the child lives a few blocks or many miles from the school. School officials must develop innovative ways to reach parents who feel detached from the schools.

STUDENTS

Students are the most effective public relations vehicles available to the school. They carry home a large volume of school news and many parents accept their reports as absolute truth. As stated elsewhere in this book, if students are well taught, challenged and motivated and if their school experiences are exciting, they are likely to take home positive and glowing reports of the school operation. The happily adjusted child is apt to reflect a wholesome account of his school. The maladjusted child is apt to reflect discredit upon his school. Each student should be made to feel at home in the school setting so he has a feeling of being part of the family and an attitude of family pride develops.

Students who misbehave on the school grounds, on the school parking lot, at athletic events or in public areas of the community or, even, driving recklessly, create a bad image which reflects on the entire student body. Citizens often judge all young people by the raucous behavior of a few. Because of this, school officials must do all they can to minimize the above types of behavior.

Communicating With Students

In recent years, school officials have improved their communications with members of the student body. In some cases the improvement resulted from student unrest or student demonstrations.

Building principals need to budget time to be with students — to listen, to talk, to discuss. This can occur before school, after school, at noon, during passing time. Some principals visit homeroom classes for discussions and to hear student concerns. Other principals have lunch with small groups of students in order to improve communications.

Some principals have experienced success with an "intermediate-type group" to help resolve student problems. Such a group may consist of a college student majoring in psychology, a respected member of the student body, and a well-liked teacher or counselor. This type of intermediate group can, sometimes, resolve student problems before they reach the administration and before they reach larger proportions.

Superintendents of school have also found it beneficial to spend time rapping, or listening, to students. A superintendent may ask to meet with a "student advisory committee" composed of elected high school student leaders (student council officers, class presidents) along with representatives of dissident or minority groups. The latter students are usually selected by the principal in consultation with counselors and physical education teachers. The advisory committee meets with the superintendent, perhaps once a month; students are permitted to bring their concerns and questions to the superintendent in an open-discussion type meeting.

In a few districts, a student board of education is operative. The student board meets once a month with the superintendent, who, in turn, presents student resolutions to the attention of the adult board of education.

The school principal or superintendent can improve student contact through use of a "student press conference." When a big news story breaks, such as a "strike settlement" or "an open campus plan," a press conference held with reporters of the high school newspaper can be a valuable experience for both, the administrator and the students. Such a news conference provides current news for the student body and allows the principal or superintendent to develop rapport with student representatives.

Kenneth Fish, principal, Rosevelt High School, Yonkers, New York, suggests the following techniques to improve communications with students:

1. Spend more time regularly circulating about the school and talking with students;

2. Keep a real open-door policy and don't let the secretary act like a palace guard;

3. Pick six students at random for lunch in your office once each week;

4. Set up a student communications committee (some regular members, some rotating) to meet twice monthly;

5. Once every few days meet with a different gym class, discussing problems and handling questions in press conference style, until every gym class has been covered;

6. Have a town meeting with students two or three times yearly for your "state of the school" report and questions.

Fund Raising

Community resentment often occurs when students are "used" by the schools. For example, when students sell commodities, door-to-door, to raise funds or when students are used to solicit funds for charitable organizations, adverse criticism results from some citizens in the community. School officials must guard against excessive student involvement in such projects.

Students and the Community

Well planned and conducted field trips reflect positively upon the school. It is good for business people to observe school personnel in action and to see learning in action. To be most effective, the visits should be well planned and supervised so as to be least disruptive to the business being observed. The trips should be followed up with letters of thanks. Extra public relations benefits result when parents are asked to help supervise students on such trips. Parents observe a wholesome school activity and disseminate news of the trip in the community.

Some classes produce student performances as part of the learning experience. This occurs in classes such as music, debate and drama. Because of their entertainment value, the student performance is often presented to the public. The school benefits by having citizens view the final product of a learning process.

School children can be effectively used as "greeters" when visitors arrive at a school building or classroom. The students should receive proper training for this assignment, however. In addition to making visitors feel welcome, the students also learn from the greeting experience. Student guides can also be employed at open house, student productions and other school-sponsored activities.

Student Activities in the School

Some form of student government should exist at every school building — elementary as well as secondary. Student government is first a learning experience in the democratic form of government. Secondly, student participation in the operation of a school develops pride, responsibility and good morale, and these reflect in the school and in the community.

Every school — elementary and secondary — should have some form of student publication. The most common publication is the student newspaper. The learning experience of publication is the prime justification for the project; however, the secondary effect of school pride, unity and morale are also important.

CHAPTER VI

DESIGNING SCHOOL PUBLICATIONS

DESIGNING SCHOOL PUBLICATIONS

Most school districts distribute an assortment of publications in order to keep their many publics informed. Printed materials, inexpensive to produce, are available in large quantities for mass distribution and are a good one-way media. Effective design of printed materials, however, requires skill and experience.

Some publications are for the school staff, some are for the community; others, such as the board meeting summary, serve both groups. School publications are designed to, first, inform people and, second, to win friends and influence people.

Three general rules apply to school printed materials:

They should be easy to read

They should be well organized

The design should lead the reader from one idea to another.

TYPES OF PUBLICATIONS

Some typical publications produced by public schools include:

Staff Newsletter
Board of Education Meeting Summary
Community Newsletter
Staff Directory
Field Trip Booklet
New Resident Brochure
Recruitment Brochure
Board of Education Policy Booklet
Teachers' Handbook
Administrators' Handbook
Welcome to Kindergarten
How Does Our District Compare?
Special Purpose Publications

PURPOSE OF PUBLICATION

A publication must be written for a purpose — to keep the staff informed, to recruit teachers, to acquaint newcomers to the community with their schools. Some type of result or action should be expected from the publication, such as staff members become knowledgeable of the school operation. The purpose and expected results should be established before a publication is produced.

WRITING FOR AN AUDIENCE

In preparing publications, the editor must determine his audience and write what the people need to know, plus what he wants them to know. However, in most publications, the author writes "what he thinks the audience should know." Community newsletters, for example, usually contain what the school public relations specialist believes the citizens should know. The interests of the school residents are not necessarily the same as those of school officials. The same is true for the contents of a teachers' handbook. To be more effective, the writer should attempt to identify, perhaps through a questionnaire, the interests of his audience and what they want to know. Although these interests should be catered to, there is also a need to interest people in additional aspects of the school operations.

The writer must assume that his audience is completely uninformed about the subject. Most school officials assume that citizens understand the basic school operation and the basic school concepts. Most citizens, however, don't. The author must prepare his materials on the basis that the typical reader knows nothing of the subject he is developing. Therefore, everything written must be explained in detail.

Each group or public for which the publication is prepared requires a different style and level of writing. A staff newsletter, for example, is written differently than the community newsletter.

GOOD LAYOUT VS. GOOD WRITING

The effective publication has both well written material and excellent layout. Both are necessary. An eye-catching layout cannot make poorly written materials become meaningful. On the other hand, well written material may lay unread if the format doesn't stir interest. The effective publication requires good writing presented in a way to create interest.

GUIDELINES FOR WRITING

Most educators produce writing which is too complex, too abstract and too long. The following suggestions are guidelines for effective writing:

> Use a simple vocabulary — avoid educational jargon. It is much better to use short simple words rather than longer or complex terms. Rather than "clandestine," use "secret;" rather than "nebulous," use "unclear;" rather than "resource center," use "library;" rather than "articulate," use "speaks clearly."

> Although the introduction must solicit interest, it should not be lengthy.

> Use short paragraphs; long paragraphs lose readers.

Use simple sentence structure. Many educators use complex sentence structure in conversation and carry the habit to their writing.

For example, the sentence, "Additional vehicles have been developed to try to insure better two-way communications with parents," can better be stated "Attempts have been made to improve parent communications."

Not all sentences need be short, however; a balance is needed which provides an interesting style.

Personal pronouns such as: we, our and you should not be used. Materials should be written in the third person.

The writing should be concise. The writer should not attempt to cover too much material. It is better to cover one concept well than to cover a dozen concepts inadequately.

The writing should be objective; there should be no editorializing by the author.

Each sentence should be carefully analyzed: Can the sentence be simplified? Are the words easily understood? Can the sentence be stated more clearly?

ADDITIONAL HELPS IN WRITING

Use "examples" to clarify concepts. Examples can help to clarify abstract ideas.

Provide aids for skimming the publication. Not all people will have the time or interest to read all of the material. Underlined subheadings allow the reader to identify the gist of the article and allow him to determine what parts he wants to read or not read.

To draw attention to a list of statements, use numbers, check marks or asterisks before each item.

Occasionally, vary the style of writing. For example, the interview technique, using questions and answers, is effective for a newsletter.

People like to see their names in print. Whenever possible, identify persons by name. Whenever people appear in a photograph, identify them.

The following suggestions on writing techniques used in publications were developed by Dr. Harold Van Winkle, Professor of Journalism, Kent State University:

Maintain a high standard in English grammar, usage, and punctuation.

The improvement of writing is not a "sometime thing." It demands study of books and materials on the subject; a continuous alertness, including an analysis of the structure of what you read and a willingness to revise and rewrite and revise and rewrite what you write.

All writing should be copyread by someone besides the writer before it goes to the typist or typesetter; and all final material should be proofed before it goes on the duplicator or printing press.

Write for the audience. Ask yourself, "What do they want to know?"

Answer the readers' questions. In other words, make your communication as complete as need be. Do not assume that the reader knows the details.

Keep your promise. If you promise the reader four reasons, then give him four reasons, arranged in such manner that he can readily identify them.

Avoid academic language. Simplify. Make it easier to read. Don't be afraid of "writing down."

Make the lead interesting, by writing it simply and getting the news up front.

Develop the lead by explaining the key idea you have presented. Don't write a topical sentence and then run away and leave it.

When you rewrite, check for (1) expressions that can be stated simpler and (2) unnecessary words and phrases that can be eliminated. Then check to see if your explanations are clear. You may find that you need to add to what you have written. Do not be a slave to brevity. Underwriting is as much a fault as is overwriting.

A BRIEF APPEARANCE

Because the competition for the reader's time is so great, the layout of printed materials should appear to be brief. To convey brevity, the page margins should be generous and white space should be used extensively. Such layout will give the impression that the publication can be quickly read. The "brief in appearance" format is important for the one-page staff newsletter as well as for the more voluminous brochures and booklets. Even a one-page newsletter which is single spaced and lacks white space will appear wordy; and, as a result, will be discarded by many readers. If the material is double spaced and with white space, the readability will increase.

USE OF PHOTOGRAPHS

Photographs can do much to enhance school publications. However, pictures should serve a purpose by enhancing the story being told.

If possible, photos should be of natural work activity and unposed. The often seen posed shots of two people talking together, pointing at the blackboard, or working at the desk, should be avoided. Photos with two or three persons are to be preferred to those involving large numbers of people. The shots should be as close-up as possible. A page with two large pictures is usually preferred to one with five small photos. The sizes of the pictures used in a publication should be varied. The shots should be large enough that the reader does not have to squint to identify the subjects.

In preparing photos for publication, the unwanted parts are cut out or "cropped." A caption should accompany every photo; persons appearing in the picture should be identified by name.

When photographs are taken to accompany a publication or newsletter, additional prints can easily be made at a minimal cost and given to the individual shown in the photos. For example, an extra picture of a student or employee who is honored can be sent by the building principal or superintendent with a congratulatory note; such gestures are very much appreciated.

An NSPRA publication, *Putting Words and Pictures About Schools Into Print,* indicates that there are three basic situations for taking pictures: (1) speakers at meetings; (2) presentations of certificates and awards (3) coming events. The following techniques are recommended by NSPRA for obtaining good shots:

Speakers

1. Catch the speaker before or after the main event, have him simulate his address and get in close. Don't try to do close-ups of speakers during meetings.

2. Line up the speaker and a local official against a plain background. Get them talking to each other. Wait for the speaker to make a humorous or serious point and shoot.

3. Pose the speaker against a poster or notice about the meeting he's addressing. Have him look off camera with a smile.

4. Escort the speaker to the first row of the audience. Have him introduce himself to a few people and shoot away.

5. If the facilities permit, get 10 feet behind and to one side of the speaker while he is addressing the group. Wait for a good side profile view and shoot.

6. Take the speaker on a tour of the school building. Catch him in the print shop or the cafeteria or some other action-filled spot talking with teachers or students.

7. Bring a youngster from the audience to the speaker. Catch them as the speaker writes his autograph.

8. Receiver faces off-camera, holds the award; donor looks over his shoulder at it.

9. Place award on a platter and present to the receiver.

10. Stand the receiver and donor, backs to camera, holding the award so the camera can focus on it. Pose them in front of a large mirror so faces can be seen.

11. Receiver and donor hold the award at arm's length toward camera.

12. The donor kisses the receiver on the cheek, while holding award about his head or behind back.

13. If the award or gift is . shiny, have receiver look into it. Angle the camera so his face is visible in reflection, and get in close for shot.

14. Place the award upright on a table. Focus close up on it with donor and receiver in the background.

15. Get a close-up personality head shot of the receiver reacting to the presentation. Use this shot without showing the donor or award. Refer to them in the cut-line or story.

Gather together the people planning the event to be publicized and —

16. Stand them in a row, all holding a banner announcing the event in front of them.

17. Give them paint brushes and display boards. Shoot them preparing posters of the event.

18. Stand them on a ladder, with hammers and paint brushes in hand, facing the camera. Show in background a wall poster announcing the event.

19. Put printed program of event upright on table. Get close-up shot with planners in background.

20. Take planners to a classroom, playground, or lunchroom to talk to children (if event is child-oriented).

21. Seat them around a table with large appropriate object in middle of table. Shoot them touching the object, talking and laughing.

22. Seek unusually high or low angle shooting position. Place planners in row, circle, or casual grouping.

SOME MECHANICS IN PUBLICATION

The following guidelines related to the mechanics of developing publications are presented:

— The left margin of the page must always be even; if there is only one or two columns, the right margin can be irregular.

— A publication should generally be limited to two kinds of type — one type for headings and another for the text. Sans Serif type is often used for headings; Roman type for the text. Italic type is difficult to read.

— As a rule, publications should not appear too expensive. This will vary with communities. A high-income district will expect more professional appearing publications. Districts with predominantly low-income people would expect less polished publications.

— Published materials, as a rule, should be printed by a professional printer. People have more confidence in printed materials that appear professionally done. Materials which are poorly typed or badly reproduced do not gain reader interest; nor do they reflect well for the school.

— Color should be used conservatively. It is better to use one color well than to have a two-color mediocre job. Too many colors make materials appear gaudy.

— Each publication should have an attention-getting title.

— Each publication should include the full name and address of the school or school district and should be dated. It is frustrating to want additional copies of a publication or more information about its contents and to find no school name or address.

A RESOURCE FILE

Every public relations specialist should develop his own resource file of "idea materials" — outstanding booklets, brochures and newsletters produced by other schools, businesses and industries. He should send for publications which are winners in national public relations contests. Copies of interesting materials described in NSPRA newsletters and in educational journals should be requested. Business and industry publish annual reports and special reports which often contain eye-catching formats. The public relations specialist should analyze ideas from such publications and then develop his own designs.

Commercially produced art designs can be purchased in booklet form through NSPRA or through an annual subscription which can be purchased from Harry A. Volk, Box 4098, Rockford, Illinois 61110. The owner may duplicate the designs for his own publications.

PROFESSIONAL HELP

The work of a professional layout man can do much to enhance a publication. Such advice can do much for a one-page newsletter as well as for the more voluminous brochures produced by schools. Some schools are fortunate to have citizens with such expertise residing in the district; some public relations experts will even volunteer their services to the schools. In most cases, however, the service must be purchased. A cost estimate for such help should first be obtained, since some experts in the field have been known to charge exorbitant fees. The expenditure for layout help can be justified, however. The quality of the publication reflects on the schools; the schools are judged by the quality of their materials. A professional looking format will also encourage more people to read the materials.

GUIDELINES IN LAYOUT AND DESIGN

The following "do's" and "don'ts" for layout and design are suggested by Brooke Todd, Jr., Washington, D. C., consultant:

"Do's"

Do try to make your publication well-organized and easy to read — thereby creating the image of a well-organized publication.

Make your layouts and your writing produce the most interest and information possible.

Use easily readable type, without too much bold type throughout. (A publication is not a billboard.)

Use good photographs. Be sure that when several people are in a photo that it is large enough so all can be recognized. The more people in a photo, the larger it should be.

Features used in each issue, such as letters to the editor, calendar of events, should have a designed head used regularly and should appear in the same place each time.

Make every effort to have your publication reach the readers at the same time each month. It builds up anticipation rather than surprise.

"Don'ts"

Stay away from tricky layouts and fancy borders. "Arty pages," unless done by a skilled designer, detract from the printed word.

Do not use illustrations unless they are good and unless they contribute to the article. You don't need them as fillers; the white space is more desirable.

Avoid using color indiscriminately. Be conservative.

Don't use letters one under the other to spell out anything. We do not read from top to bottom, we read across from left to right. Letters were designed to be used that way.

In a multi-word title it is never advisable to put each word on a separate line, indenting each word under the other to create a staggered effect from left to right.

Never print copy over a seal or photograph. You defeat both: you can't see the seal or photograph, and you can't read the copy.

Avoid using a printer whose work is questionable, even if he is the low bidder.

Don't ever stop trying to improve your publication.

EVALUATION OF PUBLICATIONS

Occasionally, school publications should be evaluated; improvements and change should result. Suggestions can be sought from the immediate staff who work with or close by the public relations specialist – his secretary, an assistant superintendent. Constructive criticism can be sought from nearby school public relations personnel. The staff newsletter can be evaluated via a questionnaire, indicated in Figure 4.

One communications specialist evaluated his community newsletter in the following manner: Members of his public relations committee, made up of citizens and staff members, were asked to make five telephone calls of a random community sampling. Each was asked to explain that he served on the school's public relations committee and that as a citizen was helping to assess the effectiveness of the community newsletter. The following questions were asked:

Feels information is valuable   Yes   No

    Comments:

Has had opportunity to use information   Yes   No

    Comments:

QUESTIONNAIRE

Dear Reader:

To help the editor know if NEWS and VIEWS is serving your needs or not, would you please take time to answer the following few questions and return the form either through school mail or U.S. Mail to the Office of Public Informations

How thoroughly do you read NEWS and VIEWS:
   do not read
   scan material
   read thoroughly
   read thoroughly and keep for reference
   no opinion

How would you judge the coverage in NEWS and VIEWS of what other schools in the district are doing:
   less needed
   right amount
   more needed
   no opinion

Is there the right amount of items on specific district educational and pupil service programs:
   less needed
   right amount
   more needed
   no opinion

What's your feeling on items on changes in administrative rules and regulations:
   less coverage needed
   coverage about right
   more coverage needed
   no opinion

Are there too many or too few articles dealing with activities and achievements of members of the staff:
   less needed
   coverage right
   less needed
   no opinion

How would you judge the articles pertaining to general educational trends and studies:
   too much
   right amount
   too few
   no opinion

Is there enough information provided on educational resources (TV, books, audio-visuals):
   too much
   right amount
   not enough
   no opinion

Is there enough detailed information provided on the Board of Education meetings:
   too much
   right amount
   not enough
   no opinion

How do you feel about the photographs in NEWS and VIEWS:
   not enough
   right amount
   too many
   no opinion

Should there be more or less photographs of class activities in NEWS and VIEWS:
   more
   same amount
   less
   no opinion

Are articles in NEWS and VIEWS:
   too long
   about the right length
   too short
   no opinion

What about the layout of NEWS and VIEWS:
   interesting and conducive to reading
   uninteresting and not conducive to reading
   no opinion

Is the size of NEWS and VIEWS:
   handy to handle and read
   unhandy to handle and read
   no opinion

Does the color of paper used for NEWS and VIEWS:
   make the publication easy to read
   make the publication hard to read
   no opinion

Is the monthly issue of NEWS and VIEWS:
   not often enough
   often enough
   too often
   no opinion

Does STAFF UPDATE help to bridge the gap between issues of NEWS and VIEWS:
   yes
   no
   no opinion

Would information on job availability in the system be of interest to you:
   yes
   no
   no opinion

Any suggestions for specific changes or additions to NEWS and VIEWS will be welcomed by the Office of Public Information.

Figure 4 — Instrument to Evaluate Staff Newsletter

Feels a need for more information or different kinds of information Comments:	Yes	No
Feels that publications are a waste of time and money Comments:	Yes	No
Would like opportunities to discuss things with school personnel through meetings or phone calls Comments:	Yes	No

School publications can be evaluated in other ways:

Hire an outside public relations consultant.

Solicit public relations specialists from local businesses and industries to evaluate publications. Large firms which have full-time public relations staff members will lend such personnel to schools without charge.

CHAPTER VII

WORKING WITH THE NEWS MEDIA

WORKING WITH THE NEWS MEDIA

Public education is receiving greater national attention today than ever before; public education is in the national limelight like never before. This attention is related to the social problems with which society is wrestling today — social problems which have become increasingly severe and which are receiving greater public attention. Some blame educators for creating the social problems — the school, it is charged, has failed to adequately prepare youth for life. Because of the vital role public education plays in preventing social problems and in alleviating those already created, the story of education in American society is an important one. The report must be presented in interesting and exciting style. Representatives of the news media are needed to tell this story.

Representatives of the media also play an important role on the local scene. Every school district has a responsibility to keep its citizens as informed about school happenings as humanly possible. News representatives are needed for this most important job. The educator must therefore do all he can to maintain effective and positive relations with the news media.

Schools lend themselves to news stories. Citizens always seem interested in stories about boys and girls. Stories about teachers also make interesting reading. Students and teachers together make up a large number of people with potential news value. Also the program scope of the school operation is large and provides many facets for news stories.

WORKING WITH REPRESENTATIVES OF THE NEWS MEDIA

The school news reporter should be a valuable member of the school public relations team; he can make significant contributions to the program. School officials, however, must make overt efforts to make the reporter feel a part of this team.

An educational writer for a large city newspaper was known to lament: "School administrators, for the most part, act as though reporters carried a concealed bomb — they seem to want to duck behind their desks for protection from the blast. Although the typical administrator may be suspicious of reporters during regular times, prior to bond issues they are delighted to see them."

School personnel must be honest and fair with news reporters. They must show respect toward media representatives. With such treatment, news reporters will be more fair and reasonable toward school officials.

School officials are often critical of the news coverage provided by the media. However, news representatives select the content and style based on the likes or demands of society. Priorities of location and space are determined in the same way. Educators have been critical, for example, of the media giving headlines to parent picketing and student strikes while providing back page coverage for "merit scholarship winners." Instead of criticizing the news editor or hoping to reform him, the educator should uncover human interest angles about scholarship winners that make them front page news. Also, the educator can prepare students who are the adults of the future to be more selective in what they value as newsworthy, to be more discriminate in their choice of reading material, and to be aware that interest in rather than importance of a story determines where it is placed in a newspaper.

Some school administrators abhor the reporter, consider him a villain, treat him with suspicion and avoid him at all costs. Some school officials refuse to talk with representatives of the media; they require reporters to submit questions in writing which are then answered in writing. The administrator's suspicion of reporters is usually based on a previous experience when, for example, one reporter was critical of a school program or decision or, perhaps, a school incident was incorrectly interpreted.

School officials who carry grudges against media personnel will lose in the long run; their relationship with the news representatives will worsen. School personnel must tolerate critical news writing and must accept that reporters will, on occasions, distort a story. They must realize that media employees, too, have frailties, just as school people do and that if they were trained as journalists, their reporting would probably be very similar to that of the reporter covering their school.

Occasionally, the "headline" used for a school story is completely misleading. The natural tendency is to blame the school reporter. Headlines, however, are usually developed by the news editor or the copy editor. Often the reporter first sees the headline when he reads the article in print. The reporter cannot, therefore, be held accountable for headline errors.

School employees must realize that news reporters consider themselves "guardians of the community" and "watchdogs of the community financial purse." In this role they have the right and privilege to prod into any school activity, problem or decision.

The Whole Story

In the past, school administrators too often channeled only the "good news" to the media. All news, however, good and bad, must be shared with reporters. The administrator will be in a stronger position if he informs his community of a bad situation so his citizens know that he is aware of the problem and is working on it.

The school person must also tell the whole story and tell the complete truth. If the story isn't told as it is, the reporter will probably ferret out the correct information anyhow. Leveling with the reporters will build trust and respect — an important principle in press-school relations.

Helping the Media Staff

The typical news media doesn't have sufficient staffing do the job it would like to do. Like most schools, news offices are understaffed. There may not be adequate personnel to cover the educational news, or the quality of the education reporter may be lacking. Too often the school news assignment is given to the reporter with the least seniority. School officials can work around such problems by sending well-written articles accompanied with photographs of good quality. An understaffed paper is usually willing to publish a well-written newsworthy article, sometimes without revisions or only a few changes.

Being Available

School personnel should be readily available to members of the news media. When a reporter is developing a story and needs information, the school representative should be available and cooperative. If the school person should be away from his office when a call is received, he should immediately be notified of the call and should attempt to return it as soon as possible. If the school officials should be unavailable for an extended time, someone knowledgeable should speak for the absent individual.

If a school person makes himself unavailable because of a story critical of the school, the reporter will usually seek the information from other sources which might be less accurate and, possibly, even biased against the school.

School people should avoid the "no comment" reply to a reporter if at all possible. Such a response does not help to build school-press relationships.

Advance Information

Occasionally school officials can provide news representatives with confidential advance information of a coming news break. This gives the news people an opportunity to be prepared for the news, to reserve the necessary space, and if need be, to do additional research in preparation for the news story.

Getting Acquainted

A newly appointed school information officer should visit media representatives to become acquainted. An appointment should be made in advance so the news officials are prepared for the visit and so a time convenient to them is selected. During the visit, needed information can be sought: office hours, deadlines, telephoned vs. printed reports, reporters responsible for school news, types of photographs acceptable for print. The school official can also be asked if the media has had adequate access to news happenings and what could be done to expedite the flow of news to the media.

Privileges

Members of the news media who cover the schools should receive some privileges. Free admittance passes should be available to them for all school athletic events and student productions. A reserved press table should be provided for the media representatives at each board meeting. If there are several reporters covering a district, school administrators should occasionally plan a luncheon for them and discuss "how to improve school news reporting."

COMPETING NEWS MEDIA

Suburban communities are often served by a weekly newspaper plus one or two dailies published in the central city. School officials will usually show favoritism toward the local weekly — release of important news stories are timed to allow the local to scoop the story. Although such a policy is abrasive to the city news media, it is a common practice used to win the cooperation and support of the local press. In case of a big news story, however, such as a student sit-in or a teachers' strike, all news media including radio and television must receive immediate information.

If there is a morning and an evening newspaper serving the community, release times can be alternated so each newspaper will receive an equal number of first releases.

THE NEWS RELEASE

Schools usually have several methods of getting school news to its citizens: monthly newsletters, weekly student-carried newsletters, telephone chains. The local news media channels complement the vehicles used by the school. The daily newspaper, radio and television provide omnipresent avenues for broadcasting news quickly and cheaply.

Most schools have a structure or a plan for soliciting news from where most news occurs — the classroom scene. News gathered at the building level is usually channeled through a central office information person who selects and releases news articles to the media best suited for its distribution.

In some school districts, a faculty news reporter is appointed for each building who has the news-gathering responsibility. Such reporters have had limited effect. First, the teacher is too busy doing his primary job — that of teaching girls and boys. In addition, some staff reporters experience problems with reporting on peer accomplishments; occasionally, there is staff jealousy involved. A few schools have employed paid para-professionals to solicit news; others have used community volunteers. An intensive in-service program is needed for whoever is given the news-gathering responsibility. The training program should be organized by the person responsible for the school's public relations program. The 15-20 hours of instruction should include:

- identifying news sources
- interviewing techniques
- determining what is newsworthy
- use of photographs
- news writing

Instructors might include representatives of the local news media, a journalism professor, a well-known school public relations person from another district, a public relations consultant. The training program cannot terminate with the completion of the in-service program. The building reporters need to meet periodically to update skills and to discuss common problems.

A simple "news-release form" should be developed for the staff reporters. (Figure 5) Such a form enables the teacher-reporter to list the essentials of the story: time, place and event; the form can then be forwarded to the central office for dissemination. A brochure which presents guidelines on the selection and preparation of news releases is often made available to such a corps of reporters.

A "news release form" and specially designed envelope for central office releases will enhance the article sent to press, radio and television (Figure 5). An eye-catching design for the envelope and news release form is easily identified and is appreciated by members of the news media. The news release form should include name, address and telephone number of the school person to be called for clarifications and for additional information.

METHODS OF REPORTING A STORY

Generally, news releases are prepared in written form and hand carried or mailed to the media office. On some occasions, if there is a big story or a complex release, a school official might personally deliver the article to the editor. By being there in person, additional information can be provided or questions can be answered. Such a personal visit will also provide an opportunity for the information officer to visit with media officials — to improve communications and develop rapport.

A fast-breaking news story close to a deadline time will require a telephone call to the editor. If the story is big enough, the editor will request the contents by phone.

Some school stories are best produced through the interview technique: the reporter sits down with the school representative and asks questions related to a particular topic.

Typically, an editor prepares the news story related to a school project and forwards the release to the media office. How much more effective, however, if a news representative were actually at the event, wrote the story and took the pictures. A school camping story, for example, could be much more effective if the professional news reporter and photographer were at the scene to accompany the students

FACT SHEET

Route :
1. Building Principal
2. Mr. Braunsdorf
3. Dr. Holub

TEACHER _____

GRADE _____

SCHOOL _____

DATE _____

WHO is this
news release about?

WHAT is going
to take place?

WHEN is this
going to take place?

WHERE is this
going to take place?

WHY?

HOW?

(Please attach photographs if possible.)

Figure 5 — News Release Form (Building Level)

A NEWS RELEASE *from the* XENIA CITY SCHOOLS

126 E. CHURCH ST., XENIA, OHIO 45385 532-372-4416

release date _____ **time** _____ **released by** _____

Figure 6 — News Release Form (District Level)

as they boiled maple sugar. Representatives of the media should be invited to the action to report the story, whenever possible. A phone tip to the city desk or the picture desk of a newspaper or to the comparable desk of a TV or radio station may bring a media representative. The notice should be given at least a day or two in advance if possible.

Writing Techniques

The person responsible for school publications needs to maintain high standards in English grammar, usage and punctuation. For many professional educators, effective writing does not come easily — it is something that has to be worked on. Books on the subject can be studied. Preparing a good manuscript requires writing, revisions, and often complete rewriting. As material is rewritten, the author should attempt to simplify his words and sentence structure. Words and phrases not needed for the meaning of the sentence should be eliminated. In some cases, however, it may be necessary to expand a sentence or a paragraph in order to add clarification. Additional information in writing techniques is presented in chapter six (6).

GETTING INTO PRINT — SELECTING A STORY

To have an article appear in print, it must usually be a big story, or it must be important news to many people. For example, a story entitled "Students Released at 2:00 p.m. for Parent Conferences" will affect many people and should be newsworthy.

The news story must also be timely. News which happens one day must appear in the next day's edition — or it may never appear. The news media also like to have a story before an important event actually occurs. If, for example, a staff member has been invited to make an address before a national convention, the news media can be provided with excerpts of the speech several days prior to it being given. A release can be entitled "Mr. Jones, Principal of Central School, to Make Major Address." The body of the release would contain the highlights of the planned presentation.

There are other elements to look for which make a story newsworthy:

— *Location* — News which occurs in the immediate locality is more important than if it took place in a more distant location.

— *Importance* — An important person, place or event is worthy of news.

— *Significance* — Something held important by citizens is newsworthy. The state legislature voting on a state lottery is important news.

— *Unusualness* — Something different although not very significant will produce news. A truck trailer driven under a low bridge which shears off the top of the trailer will make news.

An article prepared by a principal or superintendent prior to the start of the school year which includes opening school information and advice is always timely. A series of articles can be released at the close of the school year entitled, "The Principal (Superintendent) Reviews the Year's Accomplishments."

The news editor who lacks adequate staff will seek news releases which are well-written so they can be incorporated into the newspaper or broadcast with little or no editing.

GETTING INTO PRINT — MECHANICAL ASPECTS

Each news article should indicate the time of release. In most cases news would be "for immediate release." Occasionally, a delayed date is necessary, for example, to allow the staff to be first informed. Each news release should have a short headline to identify its contents. Although the editor will probably never use the headline, it allows him to obtain a quick idea of the story content.

PHOTOGRAPHS

Photographs enhance the possibility of an article being printed. Photos should not be posed, but should be of normal or natural

115

activities. Publishers prefer a limited number of persons on a photograph; they avoid those which include a large gathering of people.

Photos usually have to be quickly developed in order to reach the media offices while they are still news. A small system doesn't have the staff or equipment to do the job and usually employs an outside developer. The photo of the class valedictorian loses value each day following graduation. It is best not to write on the back of photographs as the writing may come through. Instead, the title and identifying information should be typed on paper and attached to the photo with glue. Paper clips may damage the print.

Because of time limits, news releases are often forwarded to the news media without the benefit of photographs. To help with this problem, it is suggested that the public relations specialist develop a file of photographs of the staff leadership and board of education members. The photos are then available as needed to accompany news releases.

A metropolitan daily will often send a photographer to the scene of a newsworthy event if the photo desk is called several days in advance. Often a theatrical performance will bring a photographer if the public relations specialist can think up a human interest angle or a photogenic situation. A metropolitan daily may prefer to take its own pictures. If a student were conducting an unusual independent study project such as building a space ship, the daily would send out a photographer. On curriculum Day the Cleveland, Ohio Press sent out a photographer to Rocky River (Ohio) High School to photograph a male English instructor teaching students how to make peanut brittle. A new course that no other school in the area had tried might bring a photographer if there is a photographic angle. It is certainly worth the effort of a telephone call or a letter to obtain professional photograph service available through a metropolitan staff.

If a newspaper will not send a photographer for a story, have a staff photographer or the public relations person take pictures. In some districts, each principal is provided with a camera by the board of education. The principal is close to the action, and, if he is willing, can produce excellent photographs. In some buildings a teacher is assigned who has photography as a hobby.

AT THE NEWS MEDIA OFFICE

When the story reaches the media office, the news editor decides whether or not to use the story. If used, many times it is modified or rewritten. When the release appears in print, it may be so revised that it is unrecognizable to the author.

The school reporter cannot become upset if an article is not used or if a major portion is deleted or if it appears completely rewritten. The school official must expect a certain percentage of turndowns. This percentage varies with the reporter and with the news media, but a 30% to 50% turndown rate is not uncommon.

Occasionally, the school information officer may find his story unfairly slanted; sometimes he is incorrectly quoted; sometimes incorrect information is printed. For most such errors, it is best not to make an issue of the matter. If an error of misinterpretation is of major proportion, the school person may find it desirable to visit with the news representative in an attempt to avoid future errors. The following advice on criticizing media representatives is given by James E. Lashley, a former newsman, now serving as a school public relations specialist:

"The very definition of news dictates emphasizing the unusual, and more often than not this may turn out to be bad . . . . school people must curb the impulse to gripe or berate even if they do get stung. It may be a good idea to talk helpfully with the reporter to point out a mistake in fact or judgment, but only to prevent future errors and never to demand a retraction."

Lashley concluded, "Don't get on his back; scratch it. He may do the same for you."

SUGGESTIONS FOR WRITING NEWS RELEASES

The following suggestions are designed to produce more effective news releases:

— The release should be as brief as possible, in most cases no more than one page.

— Words should be simple. The often-used terms will serve better than the more abstract terms. For example, it is better to use "buses" than "transportation facilities;" "standardized tests" rather than "assessment activities."

—   Most citizens can handle ninth-grade-level reading materials. They prefer, however, to read a year or two below their level.

—   The first paragraph should contain the most interesting information in order to hold the reader's attention. If this paragraph lacks holding power, readers will not finish reading the release.

—   Sentence structure should be short, and as simple as possible. Avoid long paragraphs. Attempt to get the main idea at the beginning of the sentence rather than trailing at the end of the sentence.

—   When a person's name appears for the first time, it should be a complete name, such as John Smith.

—   The release should be on 8-½" x 11" paper. It should be typewritten and doubled spaced. Never send carbons or duplicated material. Use only one side of the paper. Never place more than one story on a page.

—   Do not carry a sentence over to the next page.

—   Select a short headline to identify the article and type it at the top of each additional page.

—   The story on page one should begin a third of the way down the paper to allow space for the copyreader.

—   When the article is more than one page in length, type, "more" at the bottom right of the page.

—   There should be one inch margins on both sides of the paper.

—   Conclude the story with some indicator such as: #   #   #   #

THE SUPERINTENDENT'S COLUMN

Some superintendents write a weekly or bi-weekly column on school news for the local newspaper. Such a continuous schedule can be very demanding; sometimes it may mean seeking out topics in order to write a column — which can result in mediocre content. In order to provide variety in style and content, the school head can rotate the authorship to other staff representatives and to board of education members.

The columns need to be kept brief. The topics must be explained in simple language.

THE NEWS CONFERENCE

The news conference can be effective in launching a "big news story" such as introducing a new superintendent or announcing that a levy will be placed on the ballot. The news conference should be announced a day or two in advance; the purpose of the conference should be given at the same time. Physical facilities for the conference should be adequate: a table for school officials, seating for reporters, and a pleasant room. After the news announcement, time should be alloted for questions and discussion. If a great deal of detailed information is released, a summary of the contents should be made available.

LETTERS TO THE EDITOR

Surveys indicate that the "letters to the editor" section of the newspaper has high readership. On occasion this section can be used to the advantage of the schools. If, for example, the board of education has a confrontation with the community over the firing of a teacher, other citizens supportive of the board's action, can indicate opinions through letters to the editor.

LETTERS OF THANKS

Occasionally, a newspaper or a radio or television station will sponsor a fine series of articles or broadcasts related to public education. Sometimes, an editorial appears in favor of a school program or decision. Compliments to the news media representatives are in order. A personal note written to the editor or to the reporter will be appreciated. A copy should also be sent to his immediate supervisor.

CHAPTER VIII

COMMUNICATION SKILLS

COMMUNICATION SKILLS

A school district that is to develop and maintain good public relations must make all of its publicity agents conscious of communications skills — public relations specialists, administrators, students, staff (noncertificated as well as certificated) and citizens.

This chapter contains basic information on communications which should be transmitted to administrators, staff, and students. Administrators should present it to their subordinates; teachers to students, and all the aforementioned, to the citizens.

Each individual is a communicator. Communicating means delivering a message formally or informally, consciously or unconsciously, clearly, quickly and effectively. The message must be understood; it must be persuasive and it must be truthful.

The effective communicator must know his audience, develop a message, select the receiver, choose the media, determine the feedback, and send another message if need be. For example, in a school levy telephone campaign a message must be prepared, names selected; the voice via telephone represents the media; feedback is determined by the response. If a question can't be answered, another call needs to be made.

UP AND DOWN COMMUNICATIONS

In a school, communications should go up the ladder as well as down. Too often they flow just downward — from supervisors to employees or from school officials to citizens. The one-way messages usually appear as memos, bulletins, or as oral instructions. Often the upward flow, or feedback, from the employee to his supervisor; or the citizens to the board, is lacking. Lateral communication among those of the same level (such as between elementary principals or between teachers) is also often sparse.

In upward communications, the opinions and feelings of people are sought. Employees (and citizens) are encouraged to evaluate policies and procedures and to transmit their feelings to those in authority.

Several techniques cultivate feedback: the questionnaire for students, staff or citizens; personal interviews with a sampling of a group; telephone interviews; administrator's "drop-in" hour. On questionnaires and in interviews people are asked what they like and don't like, what problems are not being attended to, what suggestions for improvement they have. Some school officials reserve a certain time each day, such as 3:00 p.m. to 4:00 p.m. as an "open door" period; no appointment is necessary. Feedback is solicited during this period.

GETTING THROUGH

Effective communication within a school district is more difficult today than it used to be. As school districts become larger due to consolidations and housing sprawls, citizens feel farther removed from the schools. As society becomes increasingly transient with families constantly coming and going in the typical community, there is a continual need to "begin from the beginning." Citizens who are bombarded by the media on ways to spend their dollars become immune to the attacks and turn off all outside messages. Scott Cutlip, who teaches at the University of Wisconsin School of Journalism and Mass Communications, claims that this bombardment by communications media and the pulling and tugging of other interests has caused most individuals to develop a protective cocoon. This invisible but very real shield causes most messages to bounce off so that the individual can live securely and undisturbed. Most messages don't get through, they only irritate.

Cutlip points out that many school systems' public relations are based on a classic formula for communication, which came into vogue during World War I, even though it is out-of-date in light of today's conditions. The formula is simple — draft a message, send it through a communication channel, and expect the recipient to take action as a result of receiving the message. Many, many school system communication programs are constructed almost entirely on this antiquated concept.

Effective communication today, says Cutlip and others, demands a kind of top level planning, support and strategy which are not apparent to any degree in most school systems. It involves the tailoring of messages to meet specific audience requirements and the careful use of the right communication channel at the right time. It develops techniques of involvement and participation, feedback and two-way communication which penetrate or unwrap the insulation of the cocoons.

CONCISE COMMUNICATIONS

Brevity is most effective in communications. A brief communication generally has time to get through, and it's usually simple enough to be understood. School people should concentrate on giving a maximum of information in the shortest time possible.

ARTICULATE COMMUNICATIONS

Whether written or oral, the communication must be presented in an articulate manner. The written message must be prepared, revised; and perhaps, revised again and rewritten again. A speech must be well prepared. As a minimum, an outline of the talk should be prepared in advance. Some people prefer to write out the entire speech, determining the introduction, message and conclusion. The presentation must be sufficiently rehearsed so that it can be presented in an articulate manner. Winston Churchill, who changed the course of history with his speeches, rehearsed them many times prior to delivery. The president of a nationally known university became unavailable two days before a major address in order to have sufficient preparation time. He often had his speech retyped as many as 12 times before being satisfied with a final copy.

Speakers occasionally need to evaluate their speeches. They can tape a practice delivery of the final talk and play it back in order to seek improvement, or a speech teacher can be asked to prepare a critique of the presentation. Is the speech laced with enthusiasm and occasionally humor? Is there adequate voice inflection? Is the speech spiced with visual aids such as charts, slides, or transparencies? Are they effective and appealing or just gimmicks to keep the audience awake? Are there simple but telling words or figures of speech like General Douglas MacArthur's "Old soldiers never die. They just fade away?"

BENEFITS OF ADEQUATE COMMUNICATIONS

The school will benefit from a policy of adequate communications prepared for the staff. If staff members are fully informed, they are able to perform more effectively. An atmosphere of either ignorance or mystique takes away from a person's desire to function at his top performance level. Where information is shared, people feel part of the team and morale is enhanced.

BARRIERS TO COMMUNICATIONS

In order to have effective communications, individuals must realize that people are different and that there is nothing wrong with being different; that differences must be respected.

Wholesome communications result when there is:

Respect for the other person and his ideas;
Understanding of the other person's point of view (empathy);
Factual information; presentation of the whole story.

Too many people "write off" or "turn off" a person who doesn't agree with them. They fail to listen thoughtfully to ideas or concepts which are contrary to their own beliefs. Communications in such cases cease to exist.

There are other barriers to communications. Racial prejudices will interfere with a free flow of information and on interpretations of the flow. Barriers also exist between persons of different socio-economic levels. For example, economics can determine the amount of formal education, type of employment and cultural experiences which a person has. A family with limited finances often will not budget funds for the formal education and cultural experiences that a family with affluence would provide. Those who have been limited in these areas do not have the base of experience with people who have had greater opportunities. Effective communications is then more difficult.

If individuals are from entirely different cultures, each must make a sincere attempt to study and understand the others' culture and values. Student and citizen participation in school programs and school life can help bring this about.

A line and staff school organization will present barriers. Those who have power because of position, such as a school administrator, can experience communication difficulties. Communication is best when people equate themselves as equals. As a result some principals encourage their teachers to call them by the first names.

The geographic origins of people may present barriers. The person from a rural area thinks and talks differently from someone of metropolitan background; his values are also different. A Californian has a different way of life than someone from Georgia. Again, student and citizen participation in the school program can help reduce such barriers.

The population of a school district is made up of a wide spectrum of mental abilities. Those at the extremes of the ability spectrum have difficulty communicating. People of high ability find it easy to talk and understand in the abstract; those of less ability are not able to communicate well in this area.

The above-mentioned communication barriers are difficult to circumvent. It is much more difficult to communicate with those who are different. Improvement can only result if an individual works at the task diligently. He must strive to understand himself as well as to understand others. He must attempt to understand differences among people and to respect those differences. People must be able to accept one another as equals in order to enjoy the fruits of open and unrestricted communication.

MISINTERPRETATIONS

The following game played at social gatherings proves how creative rumor can be. The party leader whispers a statement of fact at one end of a circle of people. Each person in the circle, in turn, whispers the message to his neighbor. When the last person receives the message he is asked to repeat it out loud. The final version is usually so different than the original that it brings a loud laugh from the guests. Misinterpretation of school information also results as it is passed orally from person to person in the school establishment.

The feedback received by a school official can also be distorted because of the levels it must pass through before reaching him. Sometimes an employee will refuse to pass on "information as it is" to his superior for fear that it may not be the kind of news he wants to hear. The employee may thus only pass on what he thinks will please his superior. Information which is so filtered takes away from effective communications.

LISTENING

Since school officials devote much time to listening to citizens, students, and employees, the following tips are presented on getting the most out of being attentive:

Don't be guilty of inadequate listening. Don't be a faker — just appear to listen while the mind is elsewhere. The half-listener wastes his own time as well as that of the speaker, for he receives an inadequate message. Evaluate the words of each speaker and identify the main ideas or concepts which he is trying to convey. For example, the school person who participates in a conference needs to concentrate on what is being said. Each word should be heard so that the full meaning and understanding can be grasped.

Appear attentive by keeping eye contact. Indicate understanding by an occasional nod of the head or word of agreement.

In a lengthy message, such as a seminar, remain attentive by taking notes on the presentation. Listening is required to search out the main points or concepts of the presentation.

NONVERBAL COMMUNICATION

Since people communicate nonverbally, the following tips can be used to read the messages. A message is conveyed in a smile, a frown, a startled look. The way a person walks, stands or sits can connote an attitude. In the course of a conversation, one of the parties glancing at the clock on the wall or at his wrist watch conveys a message. The way a person's eyes look often carries a reflection. Facial expressions carry messages. The interpretation of nonverbal gestures is an art.

The following statements related to nonverbal communications are attributed to Dr. Charles Galloway, Professor, Ohio State University. The interpretations are generalities; exceptions will always occur.

Time Talks: A person will spend large amounts of time with some people, small amounts with others, no time with others. The time given reflects priorities, the worth of a person.

Space Talks: The way furniture is arranged in an office, where people are asked to sit. A desk, for example, which faces the door indicates an openness to visitors.

Each glance has a hidden meaning — at conferences, negotiations, Board of Education meetings.

People who point their finger while talking, imply a threatening gesture. The habit should be avoided especially during crucial meetings such as negotiations or a Board of Education meeting.

The following physical movements are interpreted as nonverbal types by Dr. Galloway:

... finger on nose — sign of uncertainty; doubt

... clenched fist — defiance; resistance

... hands in pockets — unsure of oneself

... finger to jaw — pondering

... hand to heart — sincerity

. . . sitting on edge of chair — willingness to accept

. . . hands on hips — ready for action

. . . sitting on chair backwards — opposition; ready to take the offensive

. . . crossed arms — used when things aren't going right; a person seldom uses this gesture with people he is comfortable with; for example, his wife.

Teachers, by the way they look at students, according to Galloway, give recognition to those they favor. By not looking at others, they ignore them. Some students get teacher eye contact only when they are bad; this can encourage them to be disobedient to get the eye recognition which has been lacking. Students may attend a class for an entire day without receiving acknowledgment or recognition.

Teachers who use the following old-fashioned nonverbal communication techniques invite student resentment: hands on the hips; finger snapping; staring.

Students develop an art of communication-lying: a serious look which implies they are listening, working hard or seriously reading an assignment when they are not.

And finally, according to Dr. Galloway, mutual glances are a powerful influence in our culture. Individuals can communicate by eye-to-eye expressions that "you are with me"; "we agree"; "we accept each other."

CHAPTER IX

**PASSING BOND ISSUES
AND LEVIES**

PASSING BOND ISSUES AND LEVIES

Although a strong public relations program, year after year, is the best way to prepare a community to vote "yes" for a bond issue, public relations must be stepped up the year before a school issue is on the ballot. Techniques for the school issue campaign will be presented in this chapter.

Before designing the campaign, the superintendent and the board should consider these factors which affect election returns:

Relationship which the board and superintendent have established with the community

"Tax climate" of the community — how resistant citizens are to additional taxes

Recent increases in local, state or federal taxes which may embitter voters who will then vent their negative feelings on the school tax issue.

During the 1960's and 1970's, support for school issues has been on the decline and the situation continues to worsen. Many school districts which in the past had proudly proclaimed that "we've never defeated a school issue in our district" have had an issue fail.

The suggestions presented in this chapter do not guarantee success, for nothing can do that today. They do represent experiences of the author based on his communities, his boards of education, and his leadership. From this storehouse of experience each administrator can tailor a compaign to suit his district and his leadership.

PREPARATION YEARS IN ADVANCE OF THE VOTE

Preparation for a school issue should begin many years prior to the vote. If a strong public relations program has been effective over a long period of time, the transition to a campaign should be smooth and merely require an acceleration of activities.

Of the public relations practices outlined in other chapters, the following are especially important for the preparation of positive community support for schools:

Preparing future voters while still in school

An effective citizens committee

Development of positive relationship with the news media

Keeping contact with community interest groups

Keeping contact with community leaders

Use of community volunteers

Maximum "two-way" communications with the community.

PREPARING FOR THE ELECTION ONE YEAR IN ADVANCE

School officials must begin to prepare their community for the need of additional funds at least a year prior to a scheduled election. A community can often be approached for such a need through a study conducted by a school citizens' committee which culminates in a recommendation for additional funds. Or, advice on financial need may come from a "blue ribbon" committee made up of influential community bankers and businessmen. A recommendation for additional funds coming from a group other than the board of education seems to make the final board decision more palatable to the community.

Advance preparation for the community might also occur through a "Report on Your Schools Banquet" (Chapter 3), during which the administration provides statistics which clearly indicate need for additional funding.

A citizens committee in one district planned a series of community town-hall type meetings with the theme, "Know Your Schools." During the first meeting, participants divided into groups to study problem areas of their choice: finance, curriculum, staff, transportation. The second meeting included a banquet at which outside speakers participated: a state legislator, a large city superintendent, the local superintendent. From the series of meetings the need for additional funding emerged; soil was prepared for a campaign which was community-mandated and occurred a year later.

In one school district a plan was developed to determine the level of education the community would be willing to support. The study entitled "Blueprint for the 70's" was sponsored by the school's citizens' committee. A "study guide" was prepared for citizens which included basic information on the school program: finance, curriculum, staff, student achievement. The guide was produced as a joint effort on the part of the citizens' committee and the school staff. The study guide described the present school program in these areas and then presented discussion questions designed to reveal parent opinion: Is the present program satisfactory? . . .too elaborate? . . .needing improvement?

As a part of the Blueprint project, a citizens' study group was formed at each building in the district. Each principal was asked to select a chairman and a planning committee of at least 12 citizens. Three meetings were sponsored by each school. The results and recommendations were tabulated and made available to the community. The community demanded an expanded school program — a grass roots request for additional school funding.

Another district used a North Central Association evaluation of its high school as a vehicle to introduce to the community the need for additional school funds. The evaluation report indicated that, although an additional levy had recently been approved by the voters, sufficient funds for a quality school program still were not available and additional funding needed to be sought. The evaluation team was led by the dean of a neighboring state university which had high standing in the community. A summary of his evaluation was headlined in the local paper, "Quality Education Still Lacking"; the report stirred the community to investigate the school needs; soil was prepared for the next needed school issue.

SELECTING A DATE FOR THE VOTE

Two months of intensive campaign work is the minimal effort needed prior to a vote. Ideally, some planning should occur about a year prior to an election. A date which draws large numbers of voters to the polls, such as the regular November election date, can be a disadvantage. The regular election days draw the largest turnout of voters; many are uninformed and negative toward money issues. The author recalls a school issue which appeared on the ballot at the same time that a homestead proposal (property tax exemption for retirees) was voted. Older voters appeared in droves; the school issue was soundly defeated.

School officials generally favor an election date which will produce a smaller vote. Off-date elections bring a smaller turnout of voters who generally are considered better educated, more civic-minded and more likely to support school issues. Selection of dates outside regular elections, however, usually costs the district more money. Each board must decide on the best date for its own particular situation.

THE ROLE OF THE SUPERINTENDENT
AND BOARD OF EDUCATION

The school levy or bond issue campaign should be organized and operated by a citizens' committee. The Board and especially the superintendent should remain in the background where they can coordinate, encourage, and supply research data when needed. The issue can best be sold by those who have a peer relationship. School people, especially central-office personnel, may be accused of self-interest and should remain in the background. News releases should be prepared and released by lay people. Photos should center around citizens. The superintendent's public participation must be selective and limited. He may appear at a town-hall type program or on a radio talk show. The superintendent certainly should not be strapped with attending large numbers of neighborhood coffee meetings. Someone else can be just as effective or more effective; he needs this time for planning and coordinating the campaign and for educational problems.

ORGANIZING FOR THE CAMPAIGN

After the board decides that an issue is to appear on the ballot, most campaigns revolve about the citizens' committee. Some communities are fortunate to have such a group working year after year; some have to appoint one. Usually, the citizens' organization consists of an executive committee of 12-15 which does the campaign planning. Backing this group is a much larger segment which makes up the necessary work committees. The citizens' committee must represent a cross section of the community — banking, retail, industrial business, labor, real estate, professional, agriculture, religious, homemakers. Members should be influential in the community and a few known school critics should be included.

The selection of a chairman is a very crucial decision. The selected leader can make or break the committee. Sometimes he is chosen by the board; other times the committee elects its own chairman. The latter process has greater risk. If this process is used, it is safer for the superintendent or board of education president to serve as a temporary chairman for the first several meetings. This will allow time for the members to become acquainted and for natural leadership to evolve and be elected by the committee.

One of the first tasks of the executive committee is to develop a campaign strategy and a campaign calendar. The strategy usually evolves around the working committees listed on the following pages. A product of the strategy planning is an organizational chart indicating the various committees and their chairmen; a master calendar must be developed early. (Figures 7 and 8)

The possibility of the issue's success is increased with maximum citizen involvement. The committee can be expanded in several ways: Each member of the executive committee can be asked to select ten people who would serve; each of these, in turn, can select ten workers. In this way the committee can grow to include hundreds of volunteers. A second approach is to have a "Little Citizens' Committee" for each building in the district — elementary, junior high and senior high. The

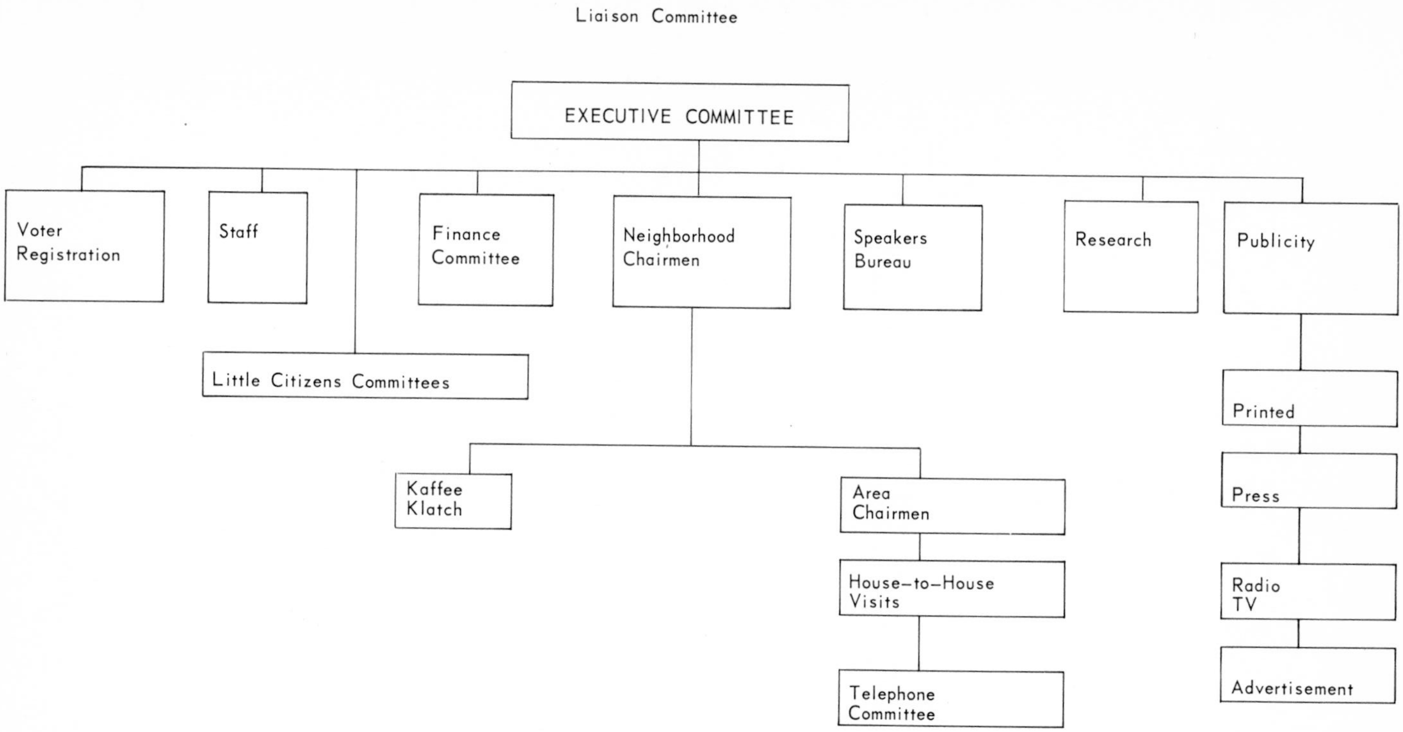

Liaison Committee

Figure 7 – Organizational Chart

EXECUTIVE COMMITTEE

Voter Registration

Staff

Finance Committee

Little Citizens Committees

Neighborhood Chairmen

Kaffee Klatch

Area Chairmen

House-to-House Visits

Telephone Committee

Speakers Bureau

Research

Publicity

Printed

Press

Radio TV

Advertisement

	Sunday	Monday	Tuesday	Wednesday	Thursday	Friday	Saturday
Sept.	6	7	8	9	10 Registration: Berea News	11 Registration: Menu News	12
	13	14	15 —List of "Little Citizens Committee" due. —Principals' In—service Meetings	16 Registration at each precinct.	17	18 Announce registration at football games—Jr. High	19
	20	21 Staff In—service Meetings—————	22	23 Registration deadline, Cleveland	24 Regular Liaison Meeting	25 ——————— ——	26
	27	28	29	30	1	2	3
Oct.	4 Newspaper ads——————————————————	5	6	7	8	9	10
	11	12	13 Home Visitors In—service Training	14	15	16	17
	18	19 Window posters Lawn Signs Kaffee Klatches begin	20	21 —————House Visit #1 ————————————————	22 Home Mailers	23	24
	25	26	27	28 ————— Home Visit #2 (for undecided voters)————— ————————————— American Education Week ——————————————————	29	30	31
Nov.	1	2 Telephone calls to Yes Voters (optional)	3 Election	Day of Thanksgiving			

Figure 8 — Levy Calendar

size of such groups can vary according to the size of the school building, but should include a minimum of 25 per building. The principal is responsible for selecting and organizing the "Little Citizens' Committee." A citizen is usually appointed as chairman; an alternate plan is to have the principal and a citizen serve as co-chairmen. To insure that the committee is appointed on time, a date should be established for the building principal to have the names and addresses of the Little Citizens' Committee membership to the superintendent. This is a highly recommended safeguard; the assignment can be difficult and it is easy to delay such tasks.

The district can be further divided into clusters. A junior high and its feeder elementary schools form a cluster. In a particular school a cluster, a citizens' group or principal may be a "laggard" and not have the motivation, leadership or ability to get the job done. Therefore, it is advisable to have a central office person assigned to each school or cluster. He can evaluate the group's progress; he has the responsibility to see that the job gets done. In a small system each principal would have to be held responsible.

A common problem of the "Little Citizens Committee": It is difficult to obtain parents to serve on the Committee. One solution is to use the class rolls for telephoning parents until a volunteer is found. Although this process may require 15 to 20 calls before someone is located — it is one way to get the job done.

A TRAINING PROGRAM

All campaign workers must know as much as possible about the issues. They will be identified with the issue, and friends will rely on them for answers. Educating the workers will require one or several training sessions. As part of this program, each person should receive a kit which contains background information, fact sheets, question-and-answer sheets.

All school personnel, certificated and noncertified, should be acquainted with basic information. Because they are identified with the school, citizens expect them to "know the answers." The building principals should be informed by the superintendent of schools; each principal, in turn, can present an informational program for his total staff. Noncertificated staff members are very influential with their groups of friends; they, too, need to be exposed to an in-service program.

CAMPAIGN SUBCOMMITTEES

The following subcommittees are suggested for possible use in a school campaign. Readers are again reminded that there is no ready-made structure for a successful campaign. Each district must determine committees, strategies and campaign materials which will best suit its unique situation.

Finance

This group must raise funds for the campaign. An estimate of the money needed for the overall campaign should be presented by the executive committee. Business and industry should be solicited first. If this group fails to contribute enough, individual and PTA contributions will be needed.

Publicity

The Publicity Committee must determine how to:

. . . . Get the facts to the voters in the most effective manner

. . . . Create a campaign theme that will appeal to voters

. . . . Establish priorities for production of campaign materials

The publicity assignment requires more time, effort and expertise than any other part of the campaign. It would be desirable if the chairman or some of his membership had professional public relations experience. Every community contains talent which can be helpful in the publicity campaign: professional public relations personnel, layout people, newspaper, radio and television personnel, photographers, advertising men and sign painters.

The release of publicity at the proper time is most important. It is possible to "shoot the works" too soon.

Good photographs, charts and graphs will usually tell the story better than words.

Finding a theme: The following methods are suggested to develop a campaign theme:

Review campaign materials from other districts.

Brain storm with professional staff, citizens committee members.

Develop a symbol — an apple, the face of a child — to go with the theme.

Fact Sheet: The fact sheet is usually presented in a question-and-answer format and presents basic facts in a simple manner. It is valuable to have for kaffee klatch meetings, house-to-house visits and speakers. Every person working in the campaign should have one.

The fact sheet will need one or several addendums — perhaps labeled "Fact Sheet No. 2," "Fact Sheet No. 3." These will contain additional questions which are presented at various community meetings.

Campaign Brochure: The brochure is one of the most important documents to be printed for the campaign; it should be mailed to each home in the community. It must be eye-catching and brief — a four-page 8-½" x 11" size will do an adequate job.

Other basic principles in preparing a brochure:

Avoid overwhelming statistics; tell the story simply.

Avoid appearing wordy; have blocks of white space.

Press Releases: Effective news releases can add to the campaign. The method of funneling such releases depends on each situation. There is a great variety of procedures demanded because each community and its press is unique. An editor in favor of the school issue can be most influential; one against the issue can be most destructive.

Small newspapers prefer to have the articles written out for them; this requires an effective writer on the committee. It is suggested that weekly newspapers receive one release per week; "dailies" receive two or three releases per week.

Better communications and rapport will result if the release is hand-delivered to the news media. A visit may also provide an opportunity for additional conversation with the editor; a question or problem may be clarified during such a visit.

Copies of news releases need to be sent to local radio and television stations. This is most important since media personnel are sensitive to being by-passed.

Representatives of the media should be invited to attend important meetings related to the issue.

Radio and television stations are usually cooperative in presenting school issues as a public service and without charge. Interviews and "talk-back" shows are effective; campaign leaders who are influential and articulate should be selected for such shows.

Campaign news can also be disseminated through special interest publications such as industrial newsletters, club bulletins and church bulletins.

Campaign personnel cannot afford to complain about the caliber or the amount of news coverage granted by the media. The media people are powerful and they can react by reducing future coverage or by eliminating it completely; or by becoming negative toward the campaign.

Paid Advertising: Paid advertising for radio, television and newspapers should be brief, simple and appealing. It should be used near the end of the campaign — the last week, perhaps.

Statements in support of the issue made by community leaders can be most effective for media advertising. Short statements made by civic leaders can tell why they will vote for the issue.

If all three media are represented in the community, paid advertising should be purchased from each of them.

Ballot Cards: Sample ballot cards can be distributed at the polls where voting machines are used. This should be done with volunteers and with no attempt to influence the voter at this time.

Printed School Programs: Printed programs passed out at plays, musicals and athletic events can serve as vehicles for school levy or bond issue information. Influential citizens often attend such functions. Brief, interesting facts and statistics such as enrollment growths, staff growth and amount spent per child for education can be presented on the back of the program or on an unused page.

Block Parties and Coffee Hours: A block party or coffee hour can be scheduled for every several blocks to tell the levy or bond issue story. These, too, require a great deal of planning, work and prodding to obtain sponsors. Members of the speakers' bureau are asked to speak at such gatherings. Some of the block parties will be very successful; some will fail. The author recalls appearing at a block party where no one attended; the meeting was a complete failure. The next evening, however, 30 citizens attended at another location. Such success extremes are normal for the block party plan. If the "Little Citizens' Committee" plan is used, block parties are planned by them.

Involving the Clergy: Members of the clergy should be invited to a meeting or a luncheon prior to the campaign; many clergymen are influential with their congregations and in their communities. The meeting can be located in a school building and, following the program, the participants can be invited to tour the school. A tour can be especially effective if a bond issue is needed to relieve the crowded conditions which they will view during the visit. Some clergymen will permit campaign literature to be distributed with the church program. They can also be asked to speak from the pulpit in suport of the issue.

The Town Hall Meeting: A "town hall meeting" might be scheduled prior to the meeting to explain the need for a school issue. The program can include:

> An inspirational talk by a citizen on the need for the school issue.

> A presentation of levy or bond issue facts,

> Small group meetings of participants to present questions and suggest ways to inform the electorate of the need for the issue.

The small group meetings will be more likely to produce results if they are led by leaders who have studied a printed discussion guide.

Other Activities:

Letters in support of the issue prepared and signed by:

>Board Members
>President, Teachers' Association
>President, retired teachers
>Union leaders (industrial)

Lawn signs
Posters for store windows
Bumper stickers
Restaurant placemats
Sample ballots
Report card inserts
A "Phone-In Night"
School literature mailed with utility bills

Credit Line: Each printed publication should conclude with a credit line which indicates the name of the sponsor and the person or group which paid for its cost.

The House-to-House Campaign

The person-to-person contact is the most effective vote-getting device available to the citizens' committee. Many citizens who discard printed materials without reading, will stop and listen to a house call. The house-to-house campaign requires much planning and a large army of workers. The school community must be divided into zones of approximately 5 square blocks. A captain is appointed for each zone; the captain of the zone solicits "home visitors" who are assigned to survey one or two blocks of homes.

An in-service program is required for the many workers involved. At this meeting workers are given the basic school background information which they need to answer questions; they are given samples of the literature which will be distributed during the visits; they are instructed on the mechanics of the visits. Role-playing can be effective as a part of the in-service program. "Playing out" visits to homes and acting out problems which might be encountered can be very beneficial to the home visitor in training.

The first visit is made two or three weeks prior to the election. A fact sheet may be distributed at this time. During the visit, the volunteer attempts to discover how the family will vote. The volunteer is instructed never to argue with a NO voter, and to never try to win over the NO vote; it is seldom accomplished. A form which indicates the residence address is marked "for," "against," or "undecided." (Figure 9) Those who indicate a NO vote do not receive a return visit. Those who are "for" or "undecided" are visited once more, perhaps a week prior to election; additional campaign material is presented to these residents; they are encouraged to turn out to vote.

The completion of the above form by the home visitor also provides assurance that the assignment was accomplished.

The importance of the home visitor conducting the interviews himself must be stressed during the training course, for some volunteers delegate the house call to their children and others skip the interviews by placing the school literature in mailboxes.

Additional steps can enable the house visit procedure to be more powerful. A month prior to the "voter registration" deadline, lists of parents of school children and their addresses can be prepared by each school. Those parents found "not registered" are visited. If they seem positive, they are encouraged to register.

During such a registration campaign, it is most surprising to find many prominent citizens and educators "not registered."

An alternate technique to the mass house-to-house visitation plan is to limit such visits to registered voters. The committee obtains the most recent list of registered voters and the house-to-house visits are only made to this group.

The get-out-to-vote campaign can be accelerated even more by the use of poll watchers. Each poll watcher is given a list of YES voters, obtained from the house-to-house visits, which are alphabetically arranged. As the voters pass the registration desk, the poll watcher notes the name and checks his list. By approximately 1:00 p.m. or 2:00 p.m., volunteers begin telephoning YES voters who have not appeared. They are urged to vote; baby-sitting services and transportation are offered.

List of voters who were contacted. See Instruction Sheet for complete directions.

Captain:

Worker:

Elementary School:

No.	Last Name	First Name	Address	Tel. No.	Probable Vote*	
					Yes	No
1						
2						
3						
4						
5						
6						
7						
8						
9						
10						
11						
12						
13						
14						
15						
16						
17						
18						
19						

*Base this answer on your conversation; do not directly ask this question. (Use "?" if you can't determine vote.)

Figure 9 — Home Visitation Form

Endorsements

Endorsements should be sought from business, civic and social groups in support of the issue. These should be sought by the chairman of the citizens' committee, the superintendent of schools or the president of the board of education. The endorsements should be requested in writing; they must receive public recognition. Periodically, a news release indicating the total endorsements and their names should be announced, such as "25 Organizations Endorse School Issue."

Speakers' Bureau

The speakers' bureau is an important phase of the campaign. It is better to have a small, able, active group which is willing to work hard than to have a large, unprepared and unreliable group. It is important that each speaker be an influential person and that he presents himself well. Each should tell the same story. To this end, the same information must be supplied to each speaker. This basic information can be made available on charts, slides, overlays or poster paper to be used on a tripod. The speaker may have his choice of visual aids, but the same facts are presented on all of the media.

A "one shot" training program for speakers can be helpful. One or two known outstanding members of the bureau can be selected to deliver a model talk on the issue.

School board members should be available for serving on this committee — they are usually well-informed and carry the prestige of their positions. Other potential candidates include ministers, attorneys and teachers.

The chairman of the speakers' bureau has an important and difficult assignment. This is especially true if "house parties" are a part of the campaign strategy. The chairman cannot afford to wait for invitations and must often solicit dates with community groups. He must schedule visual aids and arrange for their delivery.

Using Teachers and Pupils

Teachers must be used sparingly in a campaign; they should be represented proportionately, like other professions in the work expected of citizens. Their participation must be limited, especially in levy campaigns which often lead to improved salaries. Greater use includes the risk of charges, "You are campaigning for your own benefit."

The use of school children in a campaign should be limited. Although many districts have used students without controversy, a risk prevails that charges of "using children" will result from opponents.

When There Is Opposition:

When there is overt opposition, it must be ignored as much as possible. It is best to keep the campaign on a positive position; avoid becoming defensive. The news media would like nothing more than to have school officials give battle with the opposition; the school can do nothing but lose. School leaders must stay with the campaign plan and disseminate positive information. The opposition may wait until the very last minute and their literature will arrive the day prior to election so as to avoid counteraction to their statements. It is difficult to combat such a tactic. Usually the charges are false. A telephone campaign can have some effect in neutralizing the negative message.

A "VOTER'S CHOICE AT THE POLLS"

Several districts have allowed voters a choice in the level of funding for their schools. For example, two amounts appear on the ballot — 3 mills will allow schools to operate on State minimum standards; 6 mills will allow schools to operate on the present level. School officials need to spell out what each amount will buy. Voters are asked to vote affirmatively for one of the issues. Occasionally, both amounts are approved; the board is then committed to levy only the higher of the two issues.

ADDITIONAL CAMPAIGN TECHNIQUES

Campaign planners should schedule extra time and attention for groups known to be good school supporters. The following priority list indicates in descending order the level of school issue backing:

> Parents of preschoolers
> Parents of primary school age
> Parents of intermediate school age
> Parents of secondary school age

Parents whose children are out of school
Citizens who had no children
Retired

Campaign planners should, therefore, first tap those at the beginning of the list for their workers.

It is desirable to involve many women in the campaign. They are interested in schools and have the time to devote to conduct an effective campaign.

Campaign literature and materials should be kept on a very simple level. Many people do not understand graphs, charts, millage figures and, therefore, they should be used sparingly.

ALTERNATE TECHNIQUES

The Low-Key Campaign

Occasionally, a board is successful in conducting a low-key campaign. The theory is not to disturb or not to motivate the potential NO voters, and they will remain away from the polls. The hard sell is limited to those adults who are known to be good school supporters — the parents of preschool and elementary-age students. District-wide campaign techniques previously described in this chapter are not used. Instead, the citizens' committee only encourages the preschool and school-age parents and known positive voters to vote.

Avoiding Negative Precincts

The citizens committee can limit its campaign to precincts which have a record of good school support at the polls. Those precincts which consistently vote negatively can be completely by-passed in the campaign.

Campaign Directed by Public Relations Concern

Schools have an opportunity to "contract out" a campaign to a public relations concern. The professional public relations people will come in and plan the entire campaign. The fee can be paid in several ways: (1) the professional public relations people will solicit sufficient funds from local business and industry to pay the costs; or (2) a citizens' committee can be appointed to solicit money. Such public relations-directed campaigns have been used by school districts throughout the nation.

AFTER THE CAMPAIGN

Letters of Appreciation

Regardless of the outcome of the vote, thank-you letters should be sent to all volunteers who helped in the campaign. This should be done a day or two after the election. Letters should also be sent to newspaper, radio and television personnel who were involved. The letter should be signed by the chairman, the president of the board of education and the superintendent of schools.

Evaluation of the Campaign

Regardless of the outcome, the campaign must be evaluated after the results are known. A representative group of citizens can be invited to meet with the citizens' committee chairman and superintendent to identify the strengths and weaknesses of the campaign. In addition, an evaluative questionnaire can be sent to each member of the campaign committee.

Summary of Voting Results

A tabulation of the vote by precinct should be prepared and made available to citizens, board members and staff members. An attempt to diagnose low support areas should be made.

A Campaign File

A file made up of copies of all the materials used in the campaign should be prepared for future reference. Included should be copies of campaign literature, memos, letters and fact sheets. Such a file can be helpful to the next campaign manager or to the next superintendent of schools.

AFTER A DEFEAT

After a defeat at the polls, the board has to decide whether to re-submit the issue, and, if so, when and whether the issue is in need of modification. Several techniques can be used to obtain community feedback after the defeat:

> The board and the administrative staff can visit with community opinion leaders and community groups to "listen" to their advice and opinions. In a district served by the author, the police and fire departments were very influential. After a defeat, the board president and superintendent visited separately with representatives of each group and "listened."

> An opinion poll can be developed and distributed to the community or to a sampling of the community.

When school levies or bond issues are defeated, boards have been known to reduce the millage and re-submit a lesser amount. The author advises against this practice. Such reductions fester a credibility gap between the board and the voters; citizen reaction becomes, "I knew they didn't need that much." When a future issue appears, a similar attitude will probably prevail and the voters will be tempted to vote NO and to expect another reduction.

If a board insists on a millage reduction, however, the administration and board must describe carefully to the community what reductions will occur because of the reduced amount. For example, it can be announced that, because of the operating millage reduction from 8 to 6 mills, the school will not be able to add learning centers and 6 fewer teachers will be hired.

After a defeat of an operating levy, it may be necessary to reduce the education program or to reduce the number of staff members. Normally, such a plan of reduction is submitted by the superintendent for board consideration. Unfortunately, in the process the superintendent is labeled "the hatchet man." An alternate plan is to ask a committee of administrators or a joint committee of administrators and teachers to prepare a list of possible reductions. Or, a committee of citizens could recommend reductions. In the alternate plans, the finger of blame cannot point at any one person.

A school district which lost a levy at two consecutive elections, turned to its citizens and asked how they wanted to reduce the program. Approximately 70 volunteer citizens served on the committee; they were divided into six subcommittees. The citizens recommended that the program be reduced sufficiently to balance the budget Included in the recommendations was a demand that the one bus owned by the school to transport crippled children be discontinued.

A defeat or series of defeats can bring advantages. When a program has to be reduced, there is an opportunity to eliminate those programs which have become ineffective or stagnant or to eliminate personnel which are labeled as "ineffective." Sometimes a defeat will motivate a board to renewed efforts to become more "in tune" with the community; a defeat may "loosen" a board to allow the superintendent to try new programs which had previously been denied.

After several defeats at the polls, a board may decide to meet the financial crisis with a new policy. When it becomes evident that the district will not have sufficient money to meet its budget, an important decision must be made: (1) to operate schools on the present educational level and when funds run out to close down the school district until additional money becomes available; (2) to operate at the present educational level and borrow the necessary funds when money is exhausted; (3) to reduce the level of the educational program and reduce staff to allow operation within the budget.

Districts which have used plan No. 1 shock the community with a school close-down. Often the voters approve the next school issue, but this procedure creates bitter feelings and causes a loss of prestige for the district.

Plan No. 2 can avoid a school closing and allow standards to continue. However, an issue must be passed soon in order to pay back the loan; the plan also commits future funds to pay for the debt and the interest.

Plan No. 3 is used frequently by districts in financial difficulty. Because the largest percentage of the budget is for staff, staff reductions in this area produce significant savings. Staff reductions, however, should be made in all areas — teachers, noncertified and administration. The following are examples of reductions made by a district in financial trouble:

— Reductions in all areas of the staff (professional, non-certified, administrative)

— Elimination of:

> Staff visitation days
> Professional trips
> Field trips
> New text books
> Kindergarten program
> Paraprofessionals
> Department heads

— Reduction of

> Supplies and equipment
> School bus service
> School library services
> Extra-curricular activities
> Special areas — music, art, physical education

— Senior high students limited to 4 credits

CHAPTER X

ADVISORY BODIES

ADVISORY BODIES

Advisory bodies allow citizen and staff involvement in the school operation. Although they allow for input and advice, the final decisions must always rest with the administration and board of education. Advisory committees discussed in this chapter include the Citizens Advisory Committee, Public Relations Advisory Committee, School-Community Advisory Committee, Superintendent's Teacher Advisory Committee and Principal's Staff Advisory Committees.

CITIZENS ADVISORY COMMITTEE

Today there is greater citizen interest and concern about schools than ever before. Boards of education can ignore this body of interested citizens or they can involve them to the benefit of the schools. One way to utilize this talent is to appoint representatives to a citizens committee in order to seek their advice and assistance.

A "citizens advisory committee" is a group of citizens representative of the community which provides advice for a board of education. In some districts, the citizens committee operates continously on a year-round basis and advises the school board on other problems than school levies and bond issues. By working with a variety of school problems in addition to levies and bond issues, members of the citizens committee are able to disseminate current news and answer school-related questions. They are also able to return information — opinions, complaints, and the general tenor of the community toward school happenings.

In some communities an ad hoc citizens committee may be more effective. The committee is appointed to recommend a solution for a specific problem and then is disbanded. This approach is especially desirable in a community which has experienced past difficulties with citizen organizations.

The major function of a citizens advisory committee is to serve as a liaison between the public, the board of education and the school administration. This function can be accomplished by:

> Promoting a better and broader understanding among members of the public of the policies, plans and actions of the board of education and the school administration
>
> Soliciting and studying suggestions from the public and presenting those suggestions having merit to the appropriate persons and groups
>
> Studying and securing public reaction to contemplated action of the board of education and serving in an advisory capacity to the board upon its request
>
> Dispelling rumors and replacing misinformation with facts
>
> Studying and evaluating any proposed school legislation (local, state, national) placed on the ballot and publicizing the results of such studies.
>
> Promoting a high esprit de corps among parents, students, teachers, school officials, general public.

The following advantages result because of citizen participation in an advisory group:

Members, serving as resource people for regular board members, help them to be more effective by doing routine tasks and research assignments

Members by becoming educated about school operations, serve as information centers in the community

The board of education can use the citizens committee as a sounding board for new proposals.

In the absence of a formal citizens advisory committee, there is more danger of independent groups forming which are not representative of the community and which may have an "ax to grind." A board-sponsored citizens group will lessen the danger of such ad hoc pressure groups.

Organizing The Citizens Committee

Most citizens advisory committees are formed by a resolution of the board of education. The purpose or function of the citizens committee should be indicated in the resolution. There are several ways to select the membership. The Superintendent and Board, together, may select the initial membership. This could, however, result in a "rubber stamp" charge. An alternate technique is to select three or four highly respected community leaders and request that they recommend members for the committee. The members should represent a cross section of the community: geographic areas, socio-economic levels, ethnic groups and supporters as well as critics of the school operation. Both men and women should serve on the committee. Sometimes boards will ask each civic group to select a member for the committee. Such representatives, however, may feel obligated to represent the interests of the organizations they serve. Therefore, the author recommends that members not be selected as appointees of respective community organizations.

Operational guidelines should be established to indicate the purpose, areas of responsibility, financing and the advisory role to be played. To help eliminate misunderstanding, the guidelines should be made clear to all citizens committee members, board of education, staff, and the community.

To allow for efficient meetings, the size of the committee usually varies from twelve to twenty members. The superintendent of schools will often serve in an ex officio capacity. Also, if a member of the teachers' association participates, this position usually is ex officio.

The chairman of the citizens committee can be appointed by the board of education or the committee can select its own leadership. If the latter method is used and if it is a newly formed committee, the superintendent or board president should serve as a temporary chairman for one or two sessions. This allows the membership to become acquainted and the leadership to emerge.

An "executive committee" is usually formed composed of the chairman, past chairman, vice chairman, a representative from each major geographic area and the superintendent. The executive committee provides the leadership and direction for the group.

The citizens advisory committee should establish a regular schedule of meetings and convene at least once a month. The meeting time and place should be announced through the news media and be open to the public.

An agenda prepared by the chairman should be mailed to each member well in advance of the meeting date. Sessions should be reasonable in length. Some groups agree to a two-hour limit for meetings. If work isn't completed in that time, they return for an extra session. A time limitation for meetings helps to keep them moving and reduces the likelihood of a discussion's wandering from the subject.

The secretary who will take minutes of the meeting can be a member of the committee or a school secretary. The minutes should be duplicated and mailed to the membership as soon as possible following each meeting. Minutes should never be read at the meeting, for members need to make more constructive use of their time together.

Regular attendance is a problem for some committees. When a member is selected to serve, he should understand that regular attendance is expected. A constitutional clause on regular attendance may help. An example of such a statement follows:

> If a member misses three (3) consecutive meetings without a valid excuse acceptable to the executive committee or

without having an alternate attend for him, the member will be replaced.

Organizational Structure

The organizational structure of citizens committees varies. The simplest structure is a group of twelve to twenty citizens operating as a committee of the whole. Often the advisory committee is divided into several subcommittees or study committees which tackle various aspects of the educational program — finance, public relations, curriculum, transportation, personnel, building use. The following organizational pattern might result:

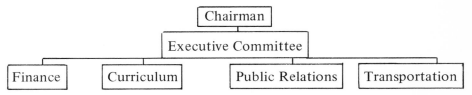

Each subcommittee would include several members of the advisory committee and, possibly, expand to include additional citizen volunteers from outside the regular membership.

The following alternate organizational structure allows for maximum citizen participation:

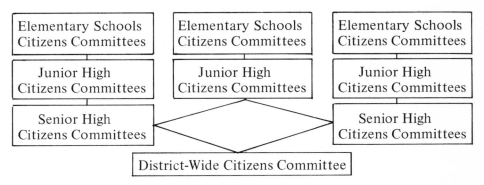

Under the above plan, each elementary attendance area has its own citizens committee. Each junior high has an advisory committee of citizens from its feeder-school attendance area. The same is true for the senior high schools. A district-wide group is also operative which receives "input" from the other committees. The advisory groups study problems related to their own school as well as district-wide problems. The structure involves risk because the large number of participants results in more opportunity for controversy.

Citizens Advisory Committees usually accomplish most of their work through subcommittee assignments. These groups, to be effective, must meet in addition to the monthly over-all meeting. The Westlake (Ohio) City School Advisory Committee formed the following sub-committees and work assignments:

1. *Public Relations:* The major task of this subcommittee is to assist the superintendent and board of education in keeping the community informed on school matters. *Classroom Commentary* (community newsletter) is one of the activities of this committee.

2. *Evaluation of the Educational Program:* This committee, which has been engaged in a long-term evaluation of the educational program, should be able to complete its work during the current calendar year and make additional specific comments and suggestions to the board of education and administration for program improvements and modification.

3. *Legislation:* This committee should be an active and, prob-ably, rather a large one. The total financial structure behind public schools is in critical straits and this committee could, and should, be actively involved in attempting to "watch dog" the General Assembly to see that school financial aid proposals are not enacted that may be detrimental to our schools without our knowledge.

4. *Extended School Year:* This committee, which will at times involve the entire S. A. C. membership, will continue its look into the prospects, feasibility, and implications of the extended school year. Included in their activities should be visits to school districts which currently have some form of an extended school year.

5. *Levy Promotion:* This subcommittee will function as a committee of the whole to help promote the renewal of an expiring operating levy plus any other necessary activities.

6. *Cooperative Arrangements With Other School Districts:* Since we are becoming more and more involved in cooperative enterprises with other school districts, this committee should serve to raise questions, seek answers, and review commitments with other school districts with which we cooperate in such endeavors as vocational education, special education, group purchasing, regional data processing and the like.

Effective Operation

All citizen committees must have a "need" if they are to exist and function effectively. Without a need, participants will become lackadaisical and half-hearted in their assignment. The board of education and administration must help identify priority problems and assignments for the committee to tackle. After the committee has identified a problem, members must agree on goals and methods of achieving them, name a date for completion, formulate a budget, and solicit funds. To build an information base, committee members should visit inside and outside the district. After observations are shared and analyzed, recommendations can be formulated.

Typical problems studied by school citizen committees include: financing, levies and bond issues, enrollment projections, curriculum, public relations, reports to parents, drug abuse, attendance lines, school questionnaires, plans for handling strikes.

Potential Conflicts

Many boards of education have avoided a permanent citizens committee for fear that it might become a second board of education and dictate or pressure the school board to act in certain ways. Unfortunately, this has happened to many boards. Several precautions need to be taken to safeguard against this danger. When the board of education establishes the citizens committee, the resolution can state that the organization can be dissolved at any time by a majority vote of the board. The superintendent, too, has a role to play. He must, when needed, remind the membership of its advisory role and warn the citizens not to move into areas reserved for administrative or board authority. An effective advisory committee must have the advice and counsel of a strong superintendent of schools.

Conflict with a board can result if the advisory committee makes a recommendation which is not followed by the board. To minimize this danger, it is suggested that recommendations be transmitted to the board through the minutes of the meeting. In this way the board is free to accept the advice which it considers useful and avoids community controversy. Any news releases concerning recommendations should be issued by the board of education and not by the advisory group.

To further minimize danger because of rejected recommendations, the board president or the superintendent should make an oral or written report to the committee showing that their findings, opinions, and suggestions have been considered. He should explain how some changes or improvements have resulted. If action on some proposals has to be delayed or if some suggestions are impractical, reasons should be given.

Some Ground Rules

Arthur Muniz, Professor at Kean College of New Jersey, Union, New Jersey, has developed ground rules for making a citizens committee work:

" 1. The advisory committee should establish a regular schedule of meetings calling for no less than one per month during the school year.

2. Regular meetings should be open to the public.

3. The school board should provide a centrally located meeting place for the committee.

4. The board should supply essential secretarial and duplicating services.

5. All committee members should receive orientation, including a tour of the schools and explanation of school operations.

6. A citizens committee should not attempt to do more work than it can handle. No more than one or two problems should be investigated by the same committee simultaneously.

164

7. Where required, services of the school board, professional staff, consultants, and other resource persons should be made available to the committee.

9. Joint meetings of the commitee and the school board should be held on some planned basis to assure close communication and cooperation.

10. All committee recommendations should be reported to the school board, never directly to the public . . . .

11. . . . Committees must confine their investigations to areas that do not impinge upon the powers and responsibilities delegated to your board by state law. Citizens committees are merely study groups — important ones, at that — and they should not be allowed to degenerate into complaint bureaus, administrative aldermen, professional ethics committees, or anything of the sort."

Sample Constitution

A sample citizens committee constitution is indicated in Appendix G.

PUBLIC RELATIONS ADVISORY COMMITTEE

A public relations advisory committee can be helpful for a principal or for a superintendent to evaluate the school's public relations program, and to make suggestions for improvement. Such a committee should represent a cross section of the staff and community: teachers, noncertificated personnel, students, citizens, professional public relations personnel, members of the local news media. The advisory group can suggest improvements in communications and in school-community relations. Instruments can be developed to evaluate school publications and other public relations media. More effective use of the news media can be recommended by the committee.

If the school district is near a large metropolitan area or near a concentration of businesses or industries, an advisory committee of public relations specialists can be formed. Many large corporations that have professional public relations staffs might as a public service release a person or two to evaluate a school public relations program. An excellent public relations review committee can be composed of several public relations experts from businesses and industries along with a public relations staff member or two from a large nearby school district.

SCHOOL-COMMUNITY ADVISORY COMMITTEE FOR THE BUILDING PRINCIPAL

Each building principal should have a school-community advisory committee. The advisory committee should represent a cross section of the school-community: teachers, noncertificated employees, students, and other citizens, golden agers. A clergyman is often a valuable member of such a group. The committee should meet periodically with the principal to suggest ways to make the school program more effective and to discuss community concerns about the schools. Such groups have been effective in reducing school vandalism by having parent patrols monitor student behavior before and after school and having schools open their doors for longer periods of time and for adult activities. Committee members must remember they are only advisors and that final decisions and authority must rest with the principal.

Success of the school-community advisory committee rests largely on the ability and the attitude of the building principal: he must be willing to (1) accept the concept of community involvement, (2) adjust to a new role based on community input, (3) acknowledge that community talent exists regardless of the socio-economic make-up. The principal must have skills in working with people. Interest and participation in such an advisory group can only be developed with a person-to-person contact. An invitation through the school newsletter will not gain significant response. Eleanor Blumenberg, Anti-Defamation League, Los Angeles, California, states that the principal must have skill in building trust, in listening and in remaining non-defensive in his dealings with the previously powerless. He must also be able to relate the limits of the groups' power: "There are clear differences between involvement and 'takeovers,' between shared decision-making and community control."

Potentially good councils also flounder, according to Blumenberg, if the principal "has too narrow a definition of the community. Whom does he see 'his' school is serving? The trick is to involve the noninvolved, hearten the dubious, and hear from the inarticulate and the alienated."

THE SUPERINTENDENT'S TEACHER ADVISORY COMMITTEE

The superintendent's teacher advisory committee, composed of a representative from each building can return valuable information to the superintendent. It can also serve a valuable function by disseminating information to the staff. Noncertificated members can serve on the committee or they can meet as a separate group with the superintendent or business manager. Representatives are selected at large at each building. To avoid a "railroad-type" election, it is best to require a minimum of two candidates for the position.

The volume of feedback information will depend on how the group is permitted to function. The superintendent can dominate the committee and thereby throttle a great deal of feedback, or he can allow participants ample time for expression, thereby expediating the flow. Members must be able to express themselves freely without fear of retaliation. If the superintendent is not able to foster such an atmosphere and freedom, only candy-coated platitudes will be expressed by the representatives.

Advisory committee sessions can help the administrator discover what is "bugging" staff members in sufficient time to avoid problems from building up into major issues. The meetings can serve as a catharsis for pent-up feelings and resentments held by staff members.

Results of the advisory meeting should be summarized and made available to the staff immediately after the sessions. A prompt summary will reduce rumors. A special format for the summary adds appearance and prestige. (Appendix H)

PRINCIPAL'S STAFF ADVISORY COMMITTEE

Each building principal should have a staff advisory committee composed of teachers to advise him in making key decisions on budget planning, curriculum problems and changes, community problems. The committee must remain advisory; the final decisions and authority are with the principal. Elementary principals usually have one teacher from each grade level; secondary principals, one from each major discipline. Such advisory groups meet at least once a month and as needed.

Faculty advisory committees have increased in numbers as a result of teacher negotiations. Advisory committees give teachers a voice in school operations even though it be advisory. Teachers' organizations hope that some of these committees can make inroads in the administration of buildings. Principals must be alert to thwart such attempts; the committee must remain strictly advisory.

The advisory committee, properly used, is an excellent administrative tool. Good principals used such teacher representation long before the era of negotiations. In good building administration teachers are involved in reviewing problems and making decisions.

It is advisable to establish such advisory groups before they are forced as a result of negotiations. If negotiated, they are considered "creatures of the association"; the negotiated structure may allow the staff to determine the members rather than allow the principal to determine the method of selection.

Other Advisory Groups

The Federal Government has required parent advisory groups in some of its legislation. Title I of Public Law 89-10 (low-income families) requires the appointment of parent advisory committees at the school district level. Vocational amendments of Public Law 90-576 require the use of industry-education advisory committees.

Such special advisory committees must have the same restraints required of a citizens advisory committee — they must limit their role to advising; they cannot dictate policy or program. The professional educator must decide what advice to accept and reject and has the responsibilities to carry out the program.

Because lay people are often not familiar with school programs, participants may be reticent and refrain from being fully involved in the work of the committee. The chairman of the advisory committee must be skilled in group dynamics so members feel comfortable to participate and to express themselves freely.

CHAPTER XI

THE PUBLIC RELATIONS DIRECTOR
AND SPECIAL GROUPS

THE PUBLIC RELATIONS DIRECTOR
AND SPECIAL GROUPS

The public relations director and school administrator must cooperate with special school-community groups. These groups contribute to both the educational program and the public relations program. Special groups presented in this chapter include the PTA, the PTA Council, Business-Industry-Education Council, Senior Citizens and other specialized community groups.

THE SCHOOL PTA

The local PTA organization can be powerful, influential and helpful in improving the school program and in working with citizens in the school community. A superintendent and principal must have positive attitudes toward PTA groups; their leadership and support are necessary to provide the foundation for successful parent-teacher organizations.

A strong building principal will usually have a strong PTA. The principal must work behind the scenes and serve as a resource person; the parents must be in the leadership role. The principal must be "behind the PTA president, and not in front of her." He must counsel and encourage his officers to plan ahead and to get things done on time

— the deadline for a budget or for next year's programs. Members must be reminded that the purpose of a PTA is to improve education, not to raise funds.

The principal must constantly suggest ways to improve the unit:

Programs should be of reasonable length.
Excellent programs should be scheduled.
A welcome should be provided for newcomers.
A printed brochure should list programs for the year.
A PTA newsletter should be published.
Methods must be tried to increase membership.

He can also facilitate PTA work by providing typing and duplicating services.

Principals should involve PTA members in the school operations:

Accompany classes on field trips.
Provide a Christmas breakfast for the staff —
    with PTA members helping to serve.
Serve as teacher volunteer helpers.
Serve as library aids

There are other ways to develop PTA leadership. In a school known to the author, the principal invites his PTA president and his or her spouse out for dinner to show appreciation for their work. In another school, the staff sponsors an appreciation dinner for the PTA officers. Some principals attend the state or national PTA convention with their presidents, which provides an opportunity to build rapport.

A superintendent can show his support for PTA by his attendance at PTA meetings. He can also verbally encourage citizens to participate in PTA activities.

THE PTA COUNCIL

The superintendent can obtain greater PTA participation and build PTA strength and influence through the development of a PTA council or congress on the district level. A PTA council is composed of one or two officers from each building PTA in the district; meetings are usually held once a month. Such councils are beneficial for several reasons:

> They provide a unifying effect for the district; representation from diverse community areas are brought together and work together.

> Projects which couldn't be undertaken by a single unit are possible because of the joining together of the units.

> They allow the superintendent to become better acquainted with the PTA leadership.

> District-wide problems can be brought to the superintendent's attention.

PTA councils operate in a variety of ways. In small districts the meetings are very informal and many amount to round-table discussions with the superintendent. Large districts hold more formal meetings with monthly programs. Councils in any size district should elect their own officers; and members should run their own meetings. Although the school administrator should attend, he should serve only as an advisor or resource person.

The school administrator can request the council to sponsor a district-wide project such as a levy campaign, community questionnaire, community seminars, a talent survey of community members. Some councils award annual scholarships; many sponsor monthly newsletters of council and unit news.

Following a PTA council meeting at which the writer was present, an influential member pulled him aside to tip him off that a teacher with an alcoholic problem was drinking in the classroom. "This is a serious charge. Are you sure of your information?", the superintendent inquired. She replied, "Oh, yes! A friend of mine actually saw the empty bottles in his room. There is no doubt that the information is correct." Because the mother was known as a purveyor of rumor, the superintendent moved quickly. Before the end of the school day, the building principal informed the mother that the teacher named in the charge was a staunch member of the Church of the Latter Day Saints and, because of his beliefs, had never indulged in drinking or smoking.

A vicious rumor was spiked because the council provided an environment for airing community problems and rumors.

BUSINESS-INDUSTRY-EDUCATION COUNCIL

Cooperation among school officials and businessmen has increased in recent years. Schools need the help which business can offer to strengthen educational programs. Business, in turn, will benefit if the schools do a better job of educating students. Better-educated graduates mean better-prepared job applicants. Businessmen are concerned about the social ferment which exists in society. Better prepared students, who have had a relevant educational experience, will provide a more stable society — something business needs for its production and for its markets.

Some school officials have been so skeptical of businessmen that a United States Health, Education and Welfare official cautioned them, "Don't get hung up looking for a welcome mat from education; educators have a certain amount of hostility to the move of big business into education." This skepticism is beginning to change, as businessmen show increased interest in community social problems. Samuel Burt, Consultant, National Advisory Council on Vocational Education. Washington, D. C., states that "The beginning of our nation's war on poverty broadened industry's perspective. It now seeks educated as well as trained employees for its offices, stores, shops and factories. The expanding social conscience of industry leads industry to conclude that we must have good schools before other ills of our urban society can be solved. Thus, the stage is set for increasing rapport between industry and education.

"Recent surveys of business attitudes toward social problems indicate industry's readiness to be involved. The National Industrial Conference Board published the results of a study of participation in public affairs by more than 1,000 companies. More than half the companies expressed willingness to initiate action to help solve socio-economic problems. Matters receiving the highest percentage of attention were those most closely related to business interests. Some of the areas concerned with education included expansion of local school facilities, problems associated with dropouts, improvement of local school curriculums and improvement of work-career opportunities for minority groups.

"Fortune Magazine asked 300 business executives this question: 'How far should business go in trying to solve social problems?' The results showed industry to be increasingly involved with social activities that go beyond the quest for profits and that some activities are far more popular than others. Support of education was rated number one.

"Industrial leaders are more anxious now than ever before to help schools because of their traumatic experiences in hiring and training large numbers of so-called disadvantaged youth and adults. They have found these people to be deficient, not only in job seeking and job-retention skills, but also in the basic fundamentals. They have found it necessary to give this type of education — as well as health and other social services — to disadvantaged new employees.

"Although industry is now able to conduct basic education programs, it would naturally prefer that such teaching be done in the schools because it has learned that prevention is much less costly than remediation."

Edward Hodges III, Assistant Vice President of the Michigan Bell Telephone Company Detroit, made the following statement to show his company's willingness to help improve education:

"There is much about education that I do not know. One thing I do know. As a businessman, I know that we in business and industry need the end products of public education. We need young men and women who have been taught to read and write and handle arithmetic. We need high-school graduates who can learn to handle our jobs. This is one reason — perhaps selfish but certainly pragmatic — why business should exert every effort to assist educators in producing well-educated graduates."

A Business-Industry-Education Council

School districts which have sizable businesses and industries should organize a "business-industry-education council" designed to promote cooperation among its members. The author invited representatives from business and industry and chambers of commerce to form such a council and was surprised at the interest and enthusiasm shown. Faculty members from the business and economics departments of a college in the area also joined.

How to Begin

How would an educator begin to plan for a business-industry-education council? First he must be familiar with the major businesses and industries in his community. He should next arrange a personal visit with the chief executives of several of the most prominent concerns to explain the business-industry-education concept. If they express interest, the school official is well on his way to success. A letter should then be prepared to a representative community group of businessmen, explaining the value of working together and inviting them to a meeting at the school office. An approximately equal number of school representatives should also be invited. An agenda should be prepared in advance. As host, the school official will chair the first meeting; a permanent chairman can be elected at a later meeting.

The first meeting which allows representatives to become acquainted should be informational. Refreshments should be available; but the session should be of reasonable length. If the meeting is too long or is allowed to ramble, representatives may not return. A first agenda usually includes:

Introductions
Purpose of a council
Review of present school-business cooperation
Discussion of potential projects

At the first meeting of the council, the following assignment can be made: each member is to suggest possible projects which the council could sponsor; the ideas are to be mailed to the chairman prior to the next meeting. The chairman then tabulates the suggestions and presents them at the next council meeting.

Care needs to be taken in selecting the first project. It should have a good chance of success and shouldn't be too time demanding on the members. This first project should be well publicized so other businessmen and the community are aware of the new venture and the benefits for school and business. Each project sponsored by the council should be carefully evaluated.

A Model

The following chart suggests an organizational structure which has functioned satisfactorily for a business-industry-education council operative in the author's district. Each district, however, needs to develop a structure which best fits its needs.

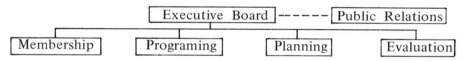

The following responsibilities are assigned to each committee:

Executive Board   — Policy-making, over-all planning,
         assignment of tasks

Membership   — Selecting and recruiting of new members to
Committee   participate in the program

Scheduling and   — Scheduling students and employees who participate
Programming   in the council's program

Planning   — Developing plans for existing and future programs;
         defining objectives

Evaluation   — Evaluating programs in terms of feasibility and
         stated objectives

Public Relations   — Publicize programs

Benefits

The school-business-industry partnership provides benefits for all involved. Among the advantages realized by the schools are:

   —   Students and faculty members become better acquainted with the world of work.

— Use of libraries, visual aids, specialized equipment owned by business and industry.

— Updating the vocational curriculum.

— Use of business and industry talent for in-service training of teachers; counseling students.

Business and industry benefit from the partnership in the following ways:

— Students (future citizens) and faculty have a better understanding of business and industry and their problems.

— School counselors can offer better vocational counseling.

— Employees benefit from adult education classes which lead to higher degrees.

Examples of Business-Industry-Education Projects

As business-industry-education partnerships increase and become more effective, exciting and valuable projects have evolved. Many benefit students; some benefit employees. In Detroit, Michigan, both the Bell Telephone Company and the Chrysler Corporation sponsor a high school. Each company offers faculty and students a variety of materials, equipment and company staff to enrich and motivate learning.

The following examples of cooperation were described in the NSPRA publication, *It Starts in the Classroom:*

"Free cooking classes were provided last summer by the Pacific Gas and Electric Company for 11- to 13-year old girls in the San Juan (Calif.) Unified School District. The company's home economist discussed meal preparation, menu planning and entertaining. The girls prepared complete meals and entertained their parents on the last day of class.

"Company house organs and industrial publications in Birmingham, Alabama, often use pictures and stories about student tours of their facilities. Local newspapers also know there is reader interest in such field trips, and devote space to them from time to time.

"An anti-dropout program, operated by the J. L. Hudson Company, a large Detroit department store, not only provides jobs for potential high school dropouts but also stresses interview techniques, proper attitudes on the job, and opportunities for getting better jobs.

"Weaver High School in Hartford, Connecticut, with 60% Negro enrollment and an overcrowded plant, has been 'adopted' by the Aetna Life and Casualty Company. Activities of the company include:

— Counseling on the operation of the school newspaper

— Field trips for the printing class

— Office-machines training on Saturdays, in the company's home office

— Photographic assistance to a class working on a photography project.

"More than 500 industrial arts projects were displayed last spring in New York City's Addressograph-Multigraph Building. Student craftsmen presented live demonstrations every day. Among sponsors of this Sixth Annual Exhibit were the Rockwell Manufacturing Company and the Varityper Corporation."

Other suggested business-industry-education council projects or activities include:

Provide post-high school counseling: Organize a group of guidance counselors, who would be available on an individual or team basis, to meet with employees at their place of employment.

Secure volunteer airline stewardesses to conduct "grace and glamor" sessions for teenage girls with emphasis on personal appearance, proper manners and acceptable social conduct.

A one-week workshop for all guidance counselors in the system in late summer for the purpose of visiting many businesses and industries in the area. The visits would acquaint them with the many types of jobs available to students.

Counseling on a "one-to-one ratio" by business representatives to motivate potential dropout students. A foreman with above average personality could be assigned three three or four junior high youths who are borderline students. He would meet with them individually and occasionally in a group. The students could visit his plant and observe the work he does. Someone showing such interest could save a potential dropout.

Additional Guidelines

Several potential problem areas are identified for school officials who are planning a partnership with business and industry. These possible pitfalls are presented in a Croft Leadership Action Folio, *Teaming Up With Industry:* (Reprinted by permission of the Publisher, Croft Educational Services Inc., New London, Connecticut.)

Starting off too low on the organizational ladder. It is important that the industrial contact be someone who can either make commitments for the firm or get to an influential person who does.

Attempting too much, too soon. Make sure that the project you suggest can reasonably be accomplished in the available time and that it has a high probability of visual success. It is much easier to go from success to success than to explain failure and be forced to start again.

Having insufficient or incomplete publicity. If you expect to develop a large base of support, it will be necessary to inform all potential members of your activity by whatever means possible. Keep in mind organization newsletters, trade journals, in-plant house organs, radio, daily, weekly and/or Sunday newspapers, bulk mailings, etc.

Inadequately preparing faculty or staff. Since a goal is a change in educators' attitudes and practices, this kind of cooperation could be strongly resisted by members of the administration or faculty who see in it a threat to their security. Conduct as many meetings as needed and send out memos as often as possible. Make sure that the key leaders and their followers realize the benefits this cooperation can bring.

Reinventing the wheel. All too often we start projects thinking that we are the only ones who ever did such a thing. This is usually incorrect and much energy is wasted duplicating previous endeavors. Take advantage of the experience of others. While each situation is unique and adaptations must be made, this is much less costly than reinventing the wheel.

Trying to impose your will on others. You are inviting people from industry who are used to being bosses and have certain expertise. This should be a cooperative venture, which means that each participant contributes his own special ability to the over-all activity. If you ask for advice and help, take it or offer logical reasons why another method is preferable, because if such assistance is ignored it will be difficult to get it again.

The preceding pages have described a business-industry-education council for a single school district. It is also possible for several contiguous school districts to join together for such a council. An even larger area can cooperate. The San Francisco Industry-Education Council covers a large metropolitan area. Even larger areas are encompassed by the Northern California Industry-Education Council; The Arizona Business-Industry-Education Council; the New York Regional Council for Industry-Education Cooperation.

SENIOR CITIZENS

Citizens who are of retirement age often feel forgotten and left out of the main stream of life. Most retirees have given many years of support to public education, both in service and in tax dollars. The schools can show appreciation for these many years of support by

181

sponsoring a Gold Card Club, which allows senior citizens to attend many school functions free of charge. The Club can be more effective if a periodic Gold Club newsletter is sent to the members which includes dates and times and locations of coming school events and an invitation to attend the functions. School programs such as short plays, musical ensembles, and art displays can be made available for Senior Citizens Club meetings. A principal or superintendent who stops to visit at such weekly meetings is graciously received.

Although a Gold Card Club is organized for the benefit of senior citizens, the author recalls planning his first Gold Card Club and receiving an admonishment from a retiree critical of the plan. The retired lady claimed that she was insulted by such a charitable offer and she would "pay my own way, thank you."

"National School Lunch Week" is often observed in school districts; students invite their parents to have a school lunch with them. Why not do the same thing for senior citizens and have "Lunch for Grandparents," allowing each child to invite a grandparent or a senior citizen?

A "Senior Citizens Day" can be sponsored by a principal or superintendent. The senior citizens are invited to the principal's office or central office for an orientation; classrooms are visited; the day is completed with a luncheon.

Schools should do more to recognize retired staff members. Too often, after years of faithful service, they retire and are forgotten. The following is a minimal plan to recognize retiring personnel:

> Retirees should be recognized at the June Board of Education meeting; they should be invited to the meeting and awarded a "certificate of appreciation" by the president of the board. Publicity in the local or school newspaper should result.

> A banquet should be held for retirees. Also invited should be staff members who have previously retired. Money to cover the cost of the banquet can be solicited from major school suppliers.

A list of all retirees and their addresses should be constantly updated.

OTHER SPECIAL GROUPS

Clergymen are usually influential citizens; they communicate with a multitude of people. It is in the interest of both, school officials and clergymen, that they be fully informed of what is happening in their schools. Therefore, periodic meetings with local ministers is very desirable. A review of recent school progress and happenings and a sharing of future plans and problems help keep these representatives informed. The chairman of the local ministerial association can serve as an advisor for planning the meeting.

A date has to be selected when the clergymen are not at a busy time.

One suburban high school allows ministers to use a counseling room once a week. Students who want help know they can see a minister that day.

Some superintendents schedule occasional informational meetings with their local barbers and beauty shop operators because schools are often discussed by their customers.

One superintendent invited the groups indicated above to meet in his most crowded building so the guests could witness the need of a bond issue which was to be placed on the ballot. Another superintendent invited his guests to meet and have lunch in a newly constructed school and followed this meeting with a tour of the new facility.

In districts where minority groups exist, a "school-community human relations council" can be helpful. Such a council is composed of influential citizens representing minority groups. Periodic meetings will allow dialogue and provide improved communications and feedback. Such sessions can reveal a potential problem in time to defuse it and avoid a disturbance or confrontation.

Santa Barbara, California, has sponsored "mini tours" of schools specifically designed for special groups such as businessmen and golden agers. Realizing that the businessmen's time is very limited, school officials developed a "mini tour" for them. Representatives are invited for 7:30 a.m. coffee and rolls during which a general orientation is presented. Tours of various school buildings follow and the program is completed by 9:00 a.m.

Many superintendents meet informally with student representatives of their secondary schools for a general discussion of student concerns. Such student forums usually meet once a month. The meetings are usually unstructured and students are permitted to speak about their problems and complaints and to ask questions. The superintendent can invite a different businessman each month to attend the forum. There are several advantages to inviting such representatives: the businessman observes the high school in action (this helps to counter rumors about the pandemonium at the high school, which often circulate in a community); he is introduced to a cross section of the student body; he hears the concerns of today's students.

CHAPTER XII

COMMUNITY SEMINARS

COMMUNITY SEMINARS

The community seminar effectively involves large numbers of citizens in a school study and provides the board of education and the administration with an excellent vehicle for obtaining community feedback. Seminars sponsored by the Columbus, Ohio, Board of Education have received national recognition. Many smaller districts have also conducted successful seminars.

PURPOSE OF SEMINARS

There are several purposes for planning community seminars. They allow citizens to:

> broaden their knowledge and understanding of existing school programs and services,

> become aware of present and future needs of the district, and

> recommend changes, improvements and broadening of the present school program.

187

HOW THE PLAN WORKS

The need for community seminars should be recognized by some respected group or person in the school family such as the board of education, a committee of citizens, or the superintendent. To be effective, the board of education and superintendent of schools must be enthusiastic about the plan. Seminars are usually planned and conducted by a committee of citizens. A study guide with basic information about the school program serves as a textbook or resource guide for the discussions. A series of seminars, to be held simultaneously at each building, one night a week for several weeks, is announced well in advance. Although the discussion guide suggests topics for discussion, participants may talk about other school-related topics. A secretary records citizens' reactions and suggestions. At the conclusion of the series, the secretary forwards the results to the seminar chairman. A summary of all reports is published and made available to interested citizens.

The following description of a community seminar project is based on the author's experience of developing such a plan while serving as a superintendent of schools.

GETTING STARTED

After board of education approval of the community seminars concept, a citizens' committee is usually selected to sponsor the project. A PTA Council or an ad hoc committee can also be called upon to sponsor the seminars. Regardless of what group is responsible, it should represent a cross section of citizens comprizing the school community. The Seminar Committee needs to (1) establish a basic policy of operation, (2) determine the basic structure of the over-all plan and (3) establish a calendar of deadlines. The Committee must also monitor the various activities, making sure that they are operating effectively and on schedule. The superintendent must provide the Committee with background information and guidance in determining the plan of action. A typical plan and calendar might include:

(Date of Completion)

Development of a Discussion Guide _____

Information Program for Administrators _____

Information Program for Teachers   ————————

Information Program for Noncertificated Employees ————————

School Steering Committee To Be Appointed   ————————

School Steering Committee to Meet (In-service)   ————————

Community Seminars   ————————

At an orientation session the Seminar Committee should learn the mechanics of the seminars, discuss the contents for a proposed guide, and select a clever title for the community seminar series. "Keys to the Future" and "Blueprint for the Future" are titles which have been used successfully.

THE DISCUSSION GUIDE

The discussion guide is the most important resource used in the community seminar project. Since the publication must be well done, funds must be provided for research and printing. A discussion guide should provide the basic background information citizens need to carry on a meaningful discussion about their schools. The guide must be written in an easy-to-read form, and information must be basic and elementary. It must be assumed that most participating citizens and staff members know very little about school operations. For example, the difference between a school operating levy and a bond issue, and other such elementary concepts must be explained in the school finance section.

Typical study topics presented in a discussion guide might include:

Pupils	Staff	Community Concerns
Instruction	Buildings	Federal and State Programs
Vocational Education	Finances	Community Services
Extended School Program	Parent Involvement	How Our School Compares

Since members of most Seminar Committees lack expertise and time to develop the discussion guide, members of the professional staff should usually be used for the task. The research and writing can be done by central office staff members or by a committee of principals and teachers who receive released time. The committee plan has the advantage of involving staff members who will carry information and enthusiasm to their buildings as well as to the community.

Although professional employees may develop a draft of the discussion guide, the revision and approval are responsibilities of the Seminar Committee.

An effective way to develop the discussion guide is to use one page for basic information on a particular program, such as "Student Personnel," followed by a page of questions which can be used to stimulate discussion. For example, the "Student Personnel" section might present enrollment growth, drop-out rates, numbers entering college, and facts concerning the special education program. Discussion questions presented on the following page could include "How can the drop-out rate be reduced?" "What plans should be made to take care of future enrollment growths?" The guide could include the topic, "The Extended School Program," and describe summer and adult programs. Related questions could include, "Should all schools remain open during evening hours for study and recreation?" "Should more schools be open evenings for students and adults in order to provide supervised study and recreation?" (See Appendix I.)

The title for the discussion guide is often the same as the one selected for the community seminar series. For example, if the seminar were given the title, "Blueprint for the Future," the discussion guide could also have the same title.

The discussion guide must have good format. Guidelines for developing publications are indicated in Chapter six (6). A guide which is too wordy or voluminous will not be read. It is desirable to have professional consultants help to develop the final format and layout.

NEED FOR INFORMATIONAL PROGRAMS
FOR DISCUSSION GUIDE

Because the contents of the discussion guide will be complicated for most school staff members and Seminar Committee members, an extensive series of informational programs or in-service programs is necessary. The members of the Seminar Committee and the school staff usually are the first to be invited to such meetings.

The Seminar Committee members and school staff will benefit from the in-service program because it will:

Allow them exposure to the guide before general distribution is made. This privilege will build teacher rapport with the committee and the administration.

Provide knowledge and enthusiasm about the project which will be passed on to the community.

Help the citizens and staff become better informed about school operations.

The following staff in-service plan was used by the author:

The first programs were held with the building principals, who were told that they would have the responsibility of providing the same information to their teaching staffs. This requirement produced additional motivation and added importance to the in-service programs. A series of four one-hour programs held for the building principals was used to explain the contents of the discussion guide. These programs, conducted by the superintendent and assistant superintendents, were taped so the principals who needed additional help could review the explanations.

Following these programs, each building principal conducted similar sessions for his staff. School was dismissed early on the four days, providing released time for the series. Secretaries and custodians attended building-level meetings. The business manager held separate classes at suitable times for bus drivers, cafeteria and maintenance personnel.

The following diagram indicates the information flow:

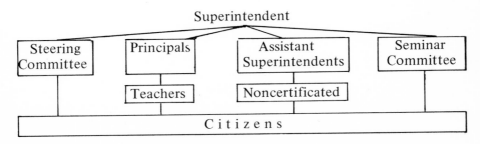

AT THE BUILDING LEVEL

A steering committee of 10 to 20 citizens was appointed for each school building. Each committee was led by co-chairmen. The principal was a co-chairman at each building and a member of the district's citizens' committee who lived in the school's attendance area was the other co-chairman. (The citizens' committee was appointed with one person living in each elementary attendance area. An alternate plan is to allow the building principal to select his own co-chairman.) The co-chairmen were instructed to use PTA representatives for no more than half of the steering committee membership. This requirement helped insure a cross-section representation of the community. The co-chairmen were asked to select, in addition to parents of present and previous students, labor and business representatives, clergymen, civic and social leaders.

All lay steering committee chairmen were invited to an in-service meeting to discuss the contents of the discussion guide. The steering committees were given basic operational instructions, but were allowed considerable autonomy to develop a plan best suited for their communities. All schools scheduled seminars at the same time: the first four Tuesday evenings in April. Location of the seminars, could be (1) at the respective school building, (2) in several homes, (3) at a house party planned by each member of the steering committee for his immediate neighborhood, or (4) a combination of these plans.

The steering committee membership (10-20 citizens) was asked to meet several times at each school prior to the seminars. In these sessions they were asked to:

Review the purpose of the community seminars.

Review the discussion guide format.

Determine the location of the seminars.

Select discussion leaders for the seminars (the principals were instructed not to serve as discussion leaders, but to be available as resource persons.)

Determine the special committees needed to implement the seminars: publicity, telephoning, refreshments.

Select a recorder who would be assigned to summarize the community seminar discussions.

Send home information via the weekly elementary school newsletter to encourage citizens to attend the community seminars.

The steering committee co-chairmen at each school were required to submit the entire list of steering committee names, including addresses and telephone numbers, by an established deadline. The listing of names was important to make sure the committee was appointed and the job done on time; the requirement also served as a prod to get the job done.

The Seminar Committee asked that the topic of "school finance" be discussed at each school seminar. Other than this, the individual steering committee selected the topics to be discussed.

COMMUNITY PREPARATION FOR THE SEMINARS

An attempt was made to provide maximum publicity for the seminars. The local press and radio were cooperative. Photographs of the citizens' committee planning the seminars ran in the newspapers several weeks before the series began. The superintendent appeared on a local radio call-in show to explain the purpose of the sessions and to encourage participation. An announcement was carried in the monthly Chamber of Commerce newsletter. Elementary students carried home reminders in their weekly newsletters. Invitations to participate were sent to the local college presidents, state and national legislators, and local and state board of education members.

All citizens were invited to attend the community seminars, regardless of whether they had children in school or not. The principals were asked to make extra efforts to involve influential citizens and opinion leaders from their respective districts. In some schools, room mothers invited parents by telephone. Elementary children wrote personal letters of invitation to their parents, grandparents, neighbors and friends. (Figure 10) Ministers were asked to encourage attendance from the pulpit, and the seminars were suggested as a topic for adult church classes. The discussion guide was used as a resource for high school social studies classes.

To: 4th, 5th, 6th Teachers
RE: "BLUEPRINT"

Suggest Each Child Write
In Own Words Two Letters
To Be Hand Delivered
To Neighbors Who Do Not
Have Children.

SAMPLE

Dear Neighbor,

The future of our schools is very important to us. We hope it is important to you, too.

Neighborhood meetings for the "Blueprints for Seventies" will be held at McKinley on April 8, 15, 21 and 28.

Please find time to come and talk about our future.

Thank you

Figure 10 — Sample Letter of Invitation

To allow for maximum publicity and to avoid confusion, four consecutive Tuesday evenings were selected for the seminars. This permitted every school in the district, elementary and secondary, to sponsor the seminars on the same dates, during the same evening hours.

THE SEMINARS

Each participant who attended a seminar received a copy of the study guide. The discussion was led by the lay co-chairmen. The principal and at least one teacher served as consultants. The meetings were limited to a length of 1½ hours. The superintendent and his assistants remained at the central office during the four consecutive evenings, answering difficult questions telephoned by principals or consultants.

After the initial session, copies of the discussion guide were placed in doctors' offices, beauty shops, barber shops and attorneys' offices.

Approximately 500 citizens in a community of 20,000 citizens participated in the series of meetings.

AFTER THE SEMINAR

After the series of four meetings was complete, recorders submitted summary reports to the chairman of the Seminar Committee. Central office staff members summarized and published the reports. A committee appointed to recommend dissemination of results suggested:

Request the local newspaper to print the results in a series of articles to last several weeks.

Develop a brochure to explain the results.

Allow citizens to discuss the results in (a) a town-hall type meeting; (b) at a PTA meeting at each school building.

A superintendent may wish to release seminar results as part of a staff in-service program or at a fall teacher-orientation program. Seminar results can also be disseminated through the staff newsletter. Information can be carried to citizens via a community newsletter mailed to each home.

The superintendent can also appoint staff study committees to make additional recommendations for implementing citizens' suggestions. Results should be considered when the school philosophy and goals are reviewed.

Many times, a community seminar results in a request by the board of education for an additional operating levy to implement the citizens' recommendations.

CHAPTER XIII

**IMPLEMENTING
A SCHOOL QUESTIONNAIRE**

IMPLEMENTING
A SCHOOL QUESTIONNAIRE

Since many citizens today seem to be turning Sherlock Holmes' magnifying glass on the schools, alert boards of education want to know what they are finding. What are they thinking about the superintendent, the principals and the teachers, the curriculum and the homework. Although their opinions are often based on facts, sometimes they are based on misinformation. The school needs to be aware of the different opinions and must be prepared to supply factual information programs when opinions are based on misinformation.

In response to this critical interest, schools are doing more than ever to communicate with their "publics" through the use of school newsletters, staff newsletters, newspaper articles, radio and television programs. These are "one-way" communication media, however, and do not provide for the needed "feedback" from the community — the thinking, opinions and evaluations of the "publics."

The school questionnaire, properly prepared, released and analyzed, can provide a valuable source of feedback information. The superintendent and board must realize that what they do *not* know know about their community's opinions may hurt them. Feedback communications, enabling the school to learn what and how much the community knows about its schools and policies and problems are necessary in today's school-conscious communities.

School surveys help a board understand how a community rates the product being turned out by the schools. The school poll may be compared to market research in the business world. The questionnaire also allows a board to find out what the community expects of its schools. The board may discover community wishes or concerns that it was unaware of. The community poll will also serve as a mirror — it will help the school realize how the community perceives it.

Results from a questionnaire provide a board of education with objective information which is needed for important decision-making. Too often boards make decisions which are influenced by pressure groups or by those not representative of the community.

A school district served by the author experienced a school bond issue defeat at the polls — a decisive 60% of the voters said "no." The Board, stunned by the defeat by a normally school-supportive community, decided to make a concentrated effort to find out precisely what had gone wrong and, hopefully, to prevent the same thing from happening again. It was decided to find out what the taxpayers really thought about the proposed building program, what they really thought about their schools in general and where the board and administrators had gone astray. The instrument for answering these questions was a carefully constructed questionnaire sent to every citizen in the district. Questionnaires were tabulated and analyzed, and the bond issue was modified based on the results of the questionnaire. When resubmitted, the issue passed with a 61% affirmative vote.

GETTING STARTED

The first step in planning a school questionnaire is to obtain board of education authorization. This can be an informal approval or in the form of a resolution. The resolution should specify the purpose of the survey. The questionnaire can be developed for a general evaluation covering the major areas of the school operation, or it can be designed for a specific area such as building needs, curriculum or school finance. The survey instrument may be used to determine the degree to which a community would accept educational innovations and change. For example, "Should school officials attempt new or innovative methods in school operations?" "If a new teaching method has been proven effective, should it be used in our schools?" The Mt. Diabo Unified School District in California developed a survey instrument specifically to determine what parents thought about their high school.

The board or superintendent must appoint a person to be responsible for the survey. Usually, this is a member of the central office staff, but in small districts it will be the superintendent of schools.

If maximum speed and efficiency in preparation of the questionnaire is desired, the director develops the questionnaire himself. However, in order to obtain the best possible instrument, members of the staff and the community should be involved in planning and executing the various phases of the project.

In a district which the author served as a superintendent, parents, teachers, board members and administrators were invited to become members of a Questionnaire Committee which developed the instrument. In addition, the board approved the use of a consultant from a local university to help the committee.

Consultant help could also have been obtained from the State Department of Education, the National Education Association or the public relations office of a local business or industry. The most valuable member of the team proved to be the university consultant who had participated in many surveys and who was able to help the committee avoid many errors.

Although a questionnaire committee (12-15 members) is more cumbersome, timeconsuming and less efficient, the rewards of greater involvement are very desirable. Advice is available from a cross section of the community and the lay members are able to help eliminate some of the professional jargon used by school people. The representatives also carried information, interest and enthusiasm about the questionnaire to the community.

Prior to the first meeting, the consultant duplicated "background information" which he had prepared on questionnaire development and distributed it to members of the committee. Consequently, the committee was able to start out with at least a general idea of where it was going and how it was going to get there. The committee found the National School Public Relations Association publication, *Feel Their Pulse,* a valuable resource booklet which provides excellent background material to prepare participants for their assignments.

DEVELOPING THE QUESTIONNAIRE

After the committee defines the areas to be included in the instrument, subcommittees determine the questions for the respective areas of the questionnaire. Prior to the next meeting of the entire committee, the subcommittee should duplicate the proposed questions and mail them to other members of the committee to encourage them to study and revise their work prior to the next session.

The proper wording of questions is an art. Prior to structuring questions, members of the committee should be urged to read NSPRA's *Feel Their Pulse* or the book, *The Art of Asking Questions,* written by Stanley L. Payne.

The purpose of a survey is to gather opinions, not to educate the community about the school operation, a task which should be reserved for other media. It is a temptation, however, to begin a question with a statement of information such as, "The average length of time from the passage of a bond issue to completed buildings is two years. The board, therefore, should propose building programs considerably in advance of anticipated needs. Yes   ; No   ; No opinion   ." The first statement is informational and should not be a part of the questionnaire.

The following is a checklist on wording questions taken from *Feel Their Pulse:*

"Try to use as few words as possible and yet have the question appear as a natural, easy flow of language.

Avoid ambiguous words.

Choose frequently used and "every day" words.

Avoid the professional educator's lingo.

Don't 'talk down.' Don't even *seem* to be talking down.

Ask questions that are within the competence of people to answer.

Use good grammar, but don't be stilted.

Be folksy, but don't use slang.

Avoid double meanings.

Word each question for one reply only. Don't try to make one question do the work of two.

Sell schools through honest questions, but don't belabor a question into a sales talk."

Developing questions should not be hurried — several months may be needed to revise and polish them properly. It is desirable to allow time for questions to "mellow" and to "shake the kinks from them." Better insights and better revisions result from allowing them to rest for a week or two prior to restudying their structure.

The question should be long enough to include all of the information essential to the study, but not so long that the respondent rejects it as being too time consuming. A short question has a better chance of being answered than a long one. The instrument may be made to appear shorter by (1) grouping similar items into sections and allowing extra space between sections; (2) using smaller type with ample spacing between items rather than using larger print with less spacing between items.

A PILOT POLL

When all areas of the questionnaire have been developed in subcommittee and revised by the entire committee, the final form should be mimeographed for use in a pilot poll of the community.

A cover letter, signed by the superintendent and board president, explaining the pilot survey and its purpose, should accompany the questionnaire. Citizens will respond more honestly if they are told not to sign the completed survey form.

Usually, the pilot sampling includes 20-30 families and members of the board of education. Those chosen for the sampling should be characteristic of the community and should include proportioned representatives of the educational, age and economic levels.

The sampling procedure proved valuable for the district served by the author. As a result some queries required rewording because, although they were understandable to the committee, they were not clear to members of the pilot group. One rather long and cumbersome question, unanswered by a significant number of the sampling group, resulted in the committee dividing the question into several shorter ones.

One of the original questions was worded, "Do you feel the maintenance of the school buildings and grounds provides for their good appearance and use?" Five citizens in the pilot poll indicated the question was unclear and they did not know what was being asked. As a result, the question was modified to read, "Do you feel our school buildings are adequately maintained?"

The pilot poll and services of the college consultant were especially valuable in revising questions.

The committee made final revisions based on the results of the pilot study and recommendations of the consultant. A cover letter explaining the purpose of the study, and which was signed by the superintendent and board president, made up the first page of the questionnaire. (Figure 11)

Since a printed instrument has a more sophisticated appearance and appears shorter than a mimeographed form, the final instrument was prepared by a printer. (Figure 12)

DISTRIBUTION OF THE QUESTIONNAIRE

Because the community of approximately 8,000 residences consists of three elementary centers, the instrument was color-coded so results could be tabulated for each respective elementary area. The questionnaire was mailed to every home by a committee of parent volunteers. The use of parents permitted additional community participation. To avoid the stigma of "junk mail," the committee

WHAT DO YOU THINK
of
YOUR SCHOOLS?

Dear Bath-Richfield Citizen:

Your Bath-Richfield Board of Education is interested in knowing what you think of our schools. Therefore, it is mailing a questionnaire to every home of the community. The results of the survey will be used by the Bath-Richfield Board of Education to make changes in the present operation of our schools and to determine the district's future educational program. Your honest opinions are requested even if you do not have children in school. Please answer as many questions as you can.

It is not necessary for you to sign the questionnaire. Some people are more likely to say what they really think if signatures are not required.

If you do not have sufficient room to complete your comments, please continue them on an additional sheet of paper and attach it to your completed questionnaire.

Please mail the completed form as soon as possible in the stamped return envelope which is enclosed.

The results of the questionnaire will be published in a future edition of the community newsletter, *Report on Your Schools*.

Your cooperation is very much appreciated.

John E. Born
President, Bath-Richfield Board of Education

Frank C. Mayer
Local Superintendent

Figure 11 — Cover Letter

School Questionnaire Bath-Richfield Local Schools

1. I have children enrolled in grades — (circle)

   K 1 2 3 4 5 6 7 8 9 10 11 12 None   Children no longer in school ☐

2. We have lived in Bath-Richfield District for the following number of years:

   1 2 3 4 5 6 More

3. Do you know as much about what is happening in the Bath-Richfield Schools as you would like?

   .... Yes   Comments: ....
   .... No   ....
   .... No opinion   ....

4. Do you feel that you are adequately informed about new programs or ideas when they are introduced into our schools? (Examples: Educational TV, modern math, etc.)

   .... Yes   Comments: ....
   .... No   ....
   .... No opinion   ....

5. Do you feel free to talk with the teachers and principals of your schools?

   .... Yes   Comments: ....
   .... No   ....
   .... No opinion   ....

6. In contacts with school personnel have you been well treated?

   .... Yes   Comments: ....
   .... No   ....
   .... No opinion   ....

7. From which of the following sources do you receive most of your information regarding the Bath-Richfield Schools? Check one or more.

   .... By my children
   .... Newspapers
   .... School publications carried by students
   .... School publications mailed to the homes
   .... Bord of Education meetings
   .... P.T.A. meetings
   .... Speakers at community meetings
   .... Others (Please specify): ....

Figure 12 — Questionnaire (Sample Page)

decided to send the instrument by first-class mail, and a return-addressed, stamped envelope (a size smaller than the mailing envelope to avoid folding) was enclosed.

Two weeks after the mailing, another group of community volunteers telephoned each fifth resident listed in the local directory to encourage returns and mailed questionnaires to those families who had misplaced their forms. According to our consultant, the return of approximately 20%, which was obtained by the survey, was about par for this type of survey.

Another committee of parents was formed to tabulate the results and to list the comments. The tabulation, however, was supervised by administrators.

The college consultant warned that the results would include harsh comments concerning school operations and school personnel. Although administrators and board members were cautioned to be prepared for critical comments, the number of them was small. Some unique, and even humorous comments were received: "Guidance people won't stay out of my boy's hair! Fashion has nothing to do with learning."

INTERPRETING RESULTS

To be effective, survey questions must be structured to bring out the good and the bad parts of school operations. The replies must be analyzed and follow-up action must be planned and carried out.

The criticisms and suggestions on school improvement are healthy indicators of an interested citizenry. Some criticisms will result from a lack of information and will indicate to the board and administration those areas where the community is in need of additional explanation.

The results of the survey, tabulated and printed in an easy-to-read bar-graph format, were mailed to the homes in the community. (Figure 13) Included with the summary was a statement assuring the people that the results and follow-up actions would be discussed in community meetings. Following a survey, it is very important that the Board put into action some of the findings and inform the community of the actions resulting because of the survey.

Report on your Schools

ISSUE 5

Bath-Richfield Schools, Bath, Ohio 44210

JUNE 1966

Tabulating results of questionnaire
Mrs. Barbara Ernshaw   Mrs. Elizabeth Wilson

WHAT DO YOU THINK
of YOUR SCHOOLS?

During May, a school questionnaire was mailed to each home in the Bath-Richfield community. Approximately 20 percent of the forms were returned. Results of the survey will be carefully studied by the Board of Education and will influence the future educational program of the District.

Because the comments were numerous and often lengthy, this report contains only those comments which appeared frequently.

The results of the questionnaire will be discussed at community meetings planned for the Fall of the year.

The Bath-Richfield Board of Education wishes to thank those of the community who completed their questionnaires.

Results of the Survey

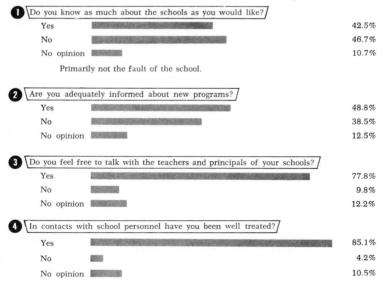

1 Do you know as much about the schools as you would like?

Yes	42.5%
No	46.7%
No opinion	10.7%

Primarily not the fault of the school.

2 Are you adequately informed about new programs?

Yes	48.8%
No	38.5%
No opinion	12.5%

3 Do you feel free to talk with the teachers and principals of your schools?

Yes	77.8%
No	9.8%
No opinion	12.2%

4 In contacts with school personnel have you been well treated?

Yes	85.1%
No	4.2%
No opinion	10.5%

Figure 13 – Results of Questionnaire (Sample Page)

5 From which of the following sources do you receive most of your information regarding the Bath-Richfield Schools?

Source	%
Children	20.4%
Newspapers	19.6%
School Publications - Students'	22.6%
School Publications - Mailers	21.4%
Board of Education Meetings	3.0%
P.T.A. Meetings	6.1%
Speakers	1.8%
Other	4.7%

6 Is the space in school buildings adequate for the educational program?

	%
Poor	12.8%
Fair	36.0%
Good	34.7%
No opinion	16.3%

Comments: Need Cafeteria at Bath, Gym at Bath, Music Room at Hillcrest

7 The older portions of the Bath and Richfield School buildings should:

	%
Remain as is	16.4%
Be remodeled	38.9%
Be replaced	21.4%
No opinion	23.1%

8 Are you satisfied that our school buildings are available for community use?

	%
Yes	80.1%
No	7.9%
No opinion	11.9%

9 Should room space be planned for future increased enrollment?

	%
Yes	66.0%
No	13.6%
No opinion	20.2%

10 Should there be a pay-as-you-go plan for a part of the building program?

	%
Yes	52.2%
No	13.5%
No opinion	34.2%

SECONDARY BENEFITS

The questionnaire experience provided several secondary benefits. Many citizens in the community praised the board for soliciting their opinions, and support for the board and the schools was generated. When people were not able to evaluate a portion of the school program, it stimulated them to ask questions to learn more about their schools. The community volunteers used to develop, mail and analyze the survey became better informed about the schools and more involved.

BOARD ACTION BASED ON QUESTIONNAIRE RESULTS

The board of education concluded from the questionnaire results that the community supported the need for additional classrooms, but questioned the need for a new high school gymnasium. The citizens approved of enlarging the industrial arts and home economics facilities. As a result, the bond issue was modified to eliminate the gymnasium and to include junior high home economics and industrial arts rooms. The issue passed with a 61% affirmative vote.

The survey also helped the board arrive at a decision on the school busing policy. Prior to the survey, elementary school students started school before secondary school students. This meant that many young children were leaving for school before it was light. The board was weighing the possibility of switching the times. The survey showed that there was no doubt about how the public felt about it; respondents favored having the high school students start school first by better than 2-1.

The survey gave the board information to support several school policies which were under fire from minority groups: For years, demands have been made upon the board to increase the number of bus pick-up points and to have buses travel down spur, or dead-end, roads to pick up pupils. The survey revealed, however, that only a distinct minority was in favor of such a change. As a result, the board took a firm stand on its bus policy and complaints slackened noticeably.

There had been community criticism about the school architect. The board thought he was doing a fine job but some people in the community thought otherwise. For years, they had kept up a drumfire of criticism against the architect — either he was too lavish in his use of materials or the hallways he designed were too wide. The survey again showed that these people represented only a *very* small minority in the community.

One of the questions which drew the greatest number of unfavorable comments was, "Are you satisfied with the foreign language program (French, Latin)? Many respondents indicated that the school should expand the language program by adding Spanish and German. Because the high school enrolled only 600 students, more than two languages could't be economically justified, however. So the board held the line despite the mandate from the public. The board's position, however, was fully explained through board and P.T.A. meetings.

The survey told the board and administration that the community wanted more school information. In response to the question, "Do you know as much about the schools as you would like?" 47% said "no." Only 43% said "yes." Another indicator of lack of knowledge was the large percentage of "no opinion" answers to specific questions about the curriculum. For example, 45% had no opinion about the guidance program, while 68% had no opinion about the operation of study halls. People lacked an opinion because they did not have enough information to form one.

As a result of such responses, the school newsletter was published every month rather than every other month. Because the respondents indicated that they didn't know if the board spent tax dollars wisely, a booklet entitled "What Does It Cost to Operate a School Program" was published.

OPINION SURVEY – ANOTHER CASE STUDY

The following unique opinion survey is presented because it differs considerably with the structure used by the author. It is described by Dr. Charles Westie of Central Michigan University, Mt. Pleasant Michigan.

"After successive bond issue defeats for new schools in the Mt. Pleasant, Michigan, School District, a group of community behavioral scientists offered their services at no cost to the board to conduct a survey of voter opinion.

"The questionnaire was based on information needed in three areas designated by the board of education

211

1. The feelings and beliefs of the electors of the district as to the various educational needs and priorities of the school district.

2. The reasons why electors had voted either for or against bond issues and rejected propositions in recent school elections.

3. Which of three tentative proposals would be most favorably received by the electors of the district.

"A questionnaire was devised, pre-tested, further revised, and then reproduced in sufficient quantity. The sample was drawn from voter registration lists, using a table of random numbers. This assured each voter an equal chance of being selected as a respondent. The entire sample of about one thousand was contacted, producing a final sample of 590 property owners. Excluded from the sample were registered voters who were not eligible electors on bond issues and persons who had moved, were deceased, or (in four cases) refused to be interviewed. The process of contacting almost 1,000 prospective interviewees called for recruiting and obtaining about 100 interviewers. The recruitment process consisted of three steps:

1. Three community residents experienced in commercial or government interviewing were found to serve as area coordinators. Each was responsible for one of the three areas into which the school district was divided for purposes of the survey. (The widespread use of sample interviewing by governmental agencies and by businesses makes it likely that persons of such training are to be found in many cities and counties.)

2. Ten interview captains were elected with the assistance of the area coordinators. All were known to be interested in community affairs and each worked under the direction of one of the coordinators.

3. Ten or more interviewers were recruited by each captain, assisted by the coordinators.

"None of the volunteer workers in this phase of the survey was selected because of any presumed attitude toward present or past school issues. There was a definite effort to represent the community as broadly as possible with regard to socio-economic status and the supervisors made a conscious attempt not to over-represent professional educators or the university community. (This would not be a problem in most communities.)

Attitude emphasized

"Interviewers and supervisors received a training manual which included objectives of the survey, background information on the nature of surveys, a description of the role of the interviewer, rather detailed instructions on locating respondents and use of the interview schedule, and discussion of special problems which might arise.

"Training sessions provided an opportunity to observe a demonstration interview, to practice asking and recording answers to schedule questions, to become familiar with the various aspects of the survey, and simply to ask questions. Respondents were assigned and materials were distributed at the training sessions.

"Both the training sessions and the manual emphasized the importance of the interviewer's attitude. Trainees were instructed not to indicate their own feelings by even slight gestures, actions or comments, any of which might cause the respondent to adjust his subsequent answers. Interviewers were instructed simply to record whatever the respondent said, regardless of their own opinions as to its accuracy, morality, pertinence, or dullness. A concluding statement in the manual read, 'We are seeking the honest, uninfluenced opinions of the voters of this school district. As an interviewer, you are simply the means by which that opinion is conveyed. Nothing of *you* should be in the interview results.'

"The interviewer training manual stressed the importance of recording answers to some questions in particular ways, and gave explicit instructions on how to probe for the 'open end' questions.

"No training efforts can guarantee the elimination of some special problems. Situations similar to the following may occur:

"Respondent refuses to allow wife to be interviewed unless he also is interviewed, even though he is not on the list to be interviewed.

"Interviewer is informed by neighbor that the respondent is a person who lives alone in a one-room house and sits with a shotgun across his knees.

"Respondent is intoxicated and refuses to be interviewed unless interviewer joins him in a drinking bout."

Interviewers found that most interviews were granted if they could locate the respondents. The number of interview refusals was limited to only four persons.

HOW ARE WE DOING?   – A ONE-PAGE QUESTIONNAIRE

While visiting a motel or a restaurant, or while traveling in a commercial airplane, customers may find a brief questionnaire entitled something like "How Are We Doing?" which allows the customer to evaluate the service or the quality of food served. Why not have such an instrument available for citizens who visit schools? Such a questionnaire designed for school use is shown in Appendix J. The questionnaire can be held in a pocket on a poster card placed on the counter of each school office. They can also be distributed to citizens in attendance at school programs or special projects. Each has a pre-printed address to the principal or superintendent. The instrument provides an excellent source of feedback.

SAMPLING

In small districts, a questionnaire is usually distributed to every resident. This procedure is referred to as a "census survey." Larger districts must resort to a sampling technique. The job of determining a scientific sample is a complex procedure, however, and requires expertise. Consultant help from a university or local business should be obtained to determine the sample. An improper sample will result in biased information. A properly constructed sample should reveal the same distribution of information as if all residents responded to the questionnaire.

THE CENSUS SURVEY VS A SAMPLING SURVEY

Advantages exist for each of the survey methods, — census and sampling. In a comparison of the two methods, Orlando Furno, Assistant Superintendent, Carroll County Public Schools, Maryland, indicates the following advantages of the census method:

Every unit to be measured has been included in the survey.

The results contain no sampling errors.

Lay persons attach greater importance to an every-person survey.

Furno lists the following disadvantages to the survey:

Census surveys cost considerably more money.

Census surveys take more time.

Census surveys require more time to complete.

Several advantages which sampling procedures have include:

Sampling is less expensive.

Sampling permits school statistics to be assessed more quickly.

Sampling increases the accuracy of the data because responses can be edited and checked more easily.

IMPROVING MAIL RETURNS

The percentage of mail-questionnaire returns can be increased through additional efforts. If the number involved in the survey is not too large, letters sent out in advance of the instrument mailing will help prepare respondents for the questionnaire. The letter must stress that their help is necessary and that the findings from the survey will be of great importance.

Leven and Gordon suggest in *Public Opinion Quarterly* that instead of sending a questionnaire directly to a member of an administrative staff, it may be more effective to forward it to the head of the organization and request that he delegate the responsibility to a member of the organization.

After a mailing, several follow-up procedures will increase returns. In spite of careful respondent preparation, a considerable number will fail to return the initial questionnaire. A follow-up mailing at a later date with another copy of the instrument should include a letter which indicates an awareness of busy schedules and encourages the respondent to complete the form. Telegrams, registered letters and telephone calls are often used as a final effort to obtain returns.

SCORING RESULTS

Most surveys are manually scored. In a large system, data processing may be desirable for scoring. This is especially true if responses are to be analyzed by school size, school type, economic level of parents or educational level of parents.

OTHER INSTRUMENTS

A Wellesley, Massachusetts, questionnaire instrument is shown in Appendix K. The questions in this survey were briefly — "yes," "no" or degree-type responses.

Other short questionnaire forms which could be incorporated in a school-community newsletter are shown in Appendix L & M.

COMMERCIAL SURVEYS

Schools can contract for the development and administration of a commercial survey. Several consulting firms will conduct opinionnaire studies for school districts. Costs are usually several thousand dollars. Such concerns often use local community volunteers to implement their plans.

CHAPTER XIV

**WORKING WITH THE COMMUNITY
AND ITS POWER STRUCTURE**

WORKING WITH THE COMMUNITY AND ITS POWER STRUCTURE

POWER

Before the school administrators responsible for public relations can relate where it counts most, they must know the community and its power structure. The power structure of a community can break a campaign for a school issue before it starts or destroy plans for a new school building before it is voted upon. Yet most administrators have not been trained to find and cultivate the power structure. This chapter will show the school administration and the public relations specialist how to become involved with the people in the community who matter the most when it comes to arousing support for schools and their issues at the polls.

KNOWING THE COMMUNITY AND ITS POWER STRUCTURE

The sociological make-up of the typical school community is very complex. Seldom is there a homogeneous population with people of similar goals and values. The few homogeneous communities that do exist are usually found in rural and isolated areas. The author once visited a small midwestern town, settled by European immigrants, which had a 98 percent Roman Catholic population. The schools although public, were staffed with members of the faith and in garb of the faith. The continued existence of such a homogeneous community structure is more difficult as the mobility of the population continues to increase and as business and industry require outside talent.

The typical population of a community is made up of many groups or publics. Each group has its own common interests and values which draw its members together. The groups or publics usually found in communities include businessmen, craftsmen, professionals, veterans, members of service organizations, parents whose children attend private or parochial schools, adults without children in school, PTA members, and press, radio, and television personnel.

Often a portion of the population does not actively participate as community members. Some commuters play and shop as well as work outside the area; another group, because the father is subject to frequent transfer, never gets into community activities.

Because communities are heterogeneous in make-up, they contain people with great variations in the values which they hold for their living and for education. Some citizens place education high on their list of values and are willing to sacrifice some modern conveniences, commercial entertainment, and personal spending in order to support better education. Other citizens, however, may give priority to such luxuries at the expense of education and resist requests for additional funds needed to improve the school program. If segments of the population polarize around divergent goals (based on values) the superintendent and board can be caught in the middle of a "tug of values."

Many educators are familiar with the affluent suburban areas which contain rambling ranch homes, three cars, a boat, and today the snowmobile, and where school financing is inadequate. One such school district known to the author, composed largely of professionals, was known to be one of the wealthiest in its county. Yet the district included the most inadequate and antiquated elementary school in the county. The teachers' work room was located in an abandoned coal bin and had no windows; there was no ventilating system in the lounge. The sub-standard conditions were presented to the voters who were living in comparative luxury but two campaigns and two elections were required to get them to approve improving the school house.

Adults who migrate to fast-growing communities were often reared in lower economic areas where education standards were lower. To such new arrivals, the school buildings and educational programs may seem very adequate or lavish when compared to their own educational experiences. The author recalls a newly arrived parent who exclaimed "What a lovely school building! You even have a room for the students to eat their lunch!" Yet, the building, one of the most out-dated in the district, having been built of spartan design as a WPA project in the early 1930's.

Community values determine the level of the educational program which the people will support. The values of the citizens also determine how fast educational innovations can be introduced. The school board or administrator who attempts to improve an educational program to a point beyond the values predominant in the community can expect citizen backlash, unrest, and criticism. Community members often will strike back with a NO vote for the next school issue or issues. The blacklash may even endanger the positions of the administrator and board members.

The administrator who changes jobs in order to advance professionally, must be able to adjust his sights or goals according to the values of the district he serves. He may one year be employed in a district which is progressive and which demands quality education, and the next year accept another position which is a promotion because of the district's size or wealth, but which has lower education standards because of the values held by the citizens. Thus a "moving administrator" must possess emotional stability to adjust to value or standard variations as he accepts leadership in a spectrum of communities.

School officials can help a community break out of its complacency by selling citizens on higher standards. Such a breakout requires a maximum amount of community involvement. For example, if a new school building is needed, officials must sell citizens in a subtle way and involve them in the planning for the new structure. Citizen excursions can be organized to visit several outstanding schools outside the district. Such visits expose parents to "higher horizons" for their children and inspire them to demand higher levels of education for their offspring. They sometimes succeed in concerning others in the community that money is needed for change.

COMMUNITY STRUCTURE

The nation's present population growth is largely limited to metropolitan areas, especially suburban centers. Since the whites have moved to the suburbs, the Negroes, Puerto Ricans, and other nonwhites have inherited more and more of the central cities.

Grace Graham *Public Schools in the American Community* (Harper and Row Publishers) identified the following communities in a typical metropolitan area:

Inner ring — directly outside the city limits.

Suburban zone — urban in characteristics and an integral part of the metropolital area.

The next general area identified by Graham is the "rural-urban fringe" which lies beyond the suburban zone. "This is the area where urban and rural forces collide, suburban industrial, and residential developments thin out and intermingle with rural villages and agricultural interests. This fringe area is in no sense homogeneous in social class." Such areas contain the seeds of potential "value problems." The ultra-conservative rural citizen finds it difficult to mesh his values with the newly arrived suburban citizen. Conflict easily results; a "tug of values" can be expected.

"CLIMATE" FOR CHANGE

A cliche often used to advise a new school administrator is to "make minimal changes during the first year of a new job; take a year to become acquainted with what you have and what you need."

It takes time for a new administrator to know how fast he can introduce change in his district. The speed of change must be governed by the "climate" which exists in the community as well as by citizens' values. If the district is satisfied with the status-quo and has been for a number of years and has an ultraconservative board of education, the administrator will have to gear his public relations program to the need for change and be patient. If, however, a board of education is willing to support change or demands change, or even hired him to bring change, a climate for improvement exists. Yet, even under the latter conditions, the speed of change must be tempered and the community must be educated to accept change. The school official will need feedback from his board, faculty, and community — has there been proper preparation for change? has change been accepted? is it too rapid?

The community which has been acclimated over a period of years toward keeping abreast educationally, is much better prepared to accept the change which is necessary to keep the educational program current. However, even such an admirable district as this needs explanation as to the reason for change and the benefits expected.

WORKING IN THE COMMUNITY

The school administrator must know his community structure. He must conduct research to obtain such information.

The basic socio-economic information can often be found from a community survey sponsored by the chamber of commerce, a regional governmental office, or a church organization. These reveal average salaries; percentage of professionals versus craftsmen; skilled laborers versus unskilled; the number of unemployed; church affiliations.

The record of school issue voting and organized opposition and support can be obtained from files of the superintendent and newspaper offices and from many old-timers.

The higher echelon administrators, including the public relations specialist, must also know the basic business, governmental, church and club operations in the community and the people who staff them. There is no substitute for personal contacts in a community. Administrators must occasionally pull themselves away from their desks and cultivate community resources such as the:

> Newspaper editor. Administrators must develop a positive relationship with the local newspaper editor and have good avenues of communication with him. He is often a member of the power structure or is familiar with the power structure. The editor knows the pulse of the community, and two-way communications with him is essential.

Chamber of Commerce. The superintendent should be a member of the chamber of commerce if one exists in his school community. The chamber allows him to make a civic contribution and to become acquainted with local businessmen.

Business and industrial leaders. It's most important for school administrators to be acquainted with the local leaders of business and industry. Occasional visits or tours of such establishments will enable the administrators to become better informed about this important segment of the community and also allow them to become familiar with owners or managers who are generally influential community members.

City and county government officials. The administrators must know and communicate with city and county officers. Not only should they be familiar with the city mayor, but also their police chief, fire chief, and other department heads. It is a good practice to visit a fire station and a police station with each chief leading the tour and making introductions. The school leadership needs to have a speaking acquaintance with county commissioners and needs to know the power structure of the county courthouse.

Ministerial association officers. Administrators must be personally acquainted with these community leaders.

President of civic clubs. School leaders should know these leaders. Their organizations need to be involved in support of school projects such as teacher orientations or breakfasts and teacher recognition day. The superintendent needs to occasionally appear before their membership as a guest speaker.

Teacher association executive committee. The superintendent needs to occasionally meet with these association representatives. He might meet with the group five or ten minutes prior to the monthly executive committee meeting to answer questions.

THE COMMUNITY POWER STRUCTURE

Every community has its power structure — the influential people who pretty well decide which way the community will vote on an issue. Most school administrators lack the knowledge to accurately analyze the community structure in order to identify those people who hold power. The study of community power structure and decision-making has become sophisticated and scientific. The comtemporary superintendent must be knowledgeable of such study techniques.

"Power" is defined by the *Dictionary of Sociology* as "the ability or authority to dominate men, to coerce and control them, and compel their action in particular ways." The term "power" can also be interpreted as the ability to move or influence other men.

Power enables a relatively few people in a community to swing important decisions, through an election for example, which effect the entire population of a community. If the power people oppose a program or issue, its chances of success are dim. Even by simply not pronouncing support for an issue, such power leaders can peril its success.

Members of the community power structure were once thought to include board of education members and presidents of civic organizations such as Rotary, Lions, Kiwanis, churches and PTA's .

However, this observation is no longer or never was accurate according to Floyd Hunter, in his book, *Community Power Structure.* His research led him to conclude:

The power structure most often includes leaders of the larger local industries, banks, law firms, commercial houses, and newspapers

Members of the power structure did not serve on school boards nor were they involved in school policy determination

Educational decisions were relegated to a lower level of power personnel

Public school administrators, college personnel, and members of the clergy are seldom represented with the power elite

Hunter discovered that the members of the true power protected themselves from excessive demands of time and energy by delegating policy execution to members of lesser power. Examples of "levels of power" identified by Hunter are:

First Level: Industrial, commercial, financial owners, and top executives of large enterprises.

Second Level: Operations officials, bank vice-presidents, public relations men, small businessmen (owners), top ranking public officials, corporation attorneys, contractors.

Third Level: Civic organization personnel, civic agency board personnel, newspaper columnists, radio commentators, petty public officials, selected organization executives.

Fourth Level: Professionals such as ministers, teachers, social workers, personnel directors, and such persons as small business managers, higher paid accountants, and the like.

Members of the first two levels "set policy;" the remaining levels carry out the policies.

Members of the power structure gained such positions because their wealth allowed them to have control of the economic level of many people. A bank official, for example, not only controls large sums of capital needed by business and industry, but he also directly (his employees) and indirectly (community business) affects salaries and positions of many people.

The power structure elite realize that there are limits to their authority. The mass population at the base of the power triangle can swing any election. This is possible because American society allows free speech, freedom of the press, and the right to organize and assemble. A vocal minority can often campaign sufficiently hard to convince either (1) the power structure or (2) if not the power structure, the large base of citizens — to support their cause.

Power influence is exerted when any major school issue is proposed. This is especially true if the plan involves additional financing. It is occasionally true that members of a community power structure doomed a school issue by deciding against it even before the school citizens committee begins its campaign. Most decisions reached by members of the power group occur in an informal atmosphere such as at lunch, garden parties, social clubs, or on the golf course. Their decisions are also disseminated through such informal gatherings.

Although many communities have a monolithic power structure, research concludes that some communities have several groups striving for power such as an "old line" group vying with an emerging youthful group which hopes to break the status-quo long held by the "old line."

IDENTIFICATION OF THE POWER STRUCTURE MEMBERS

What are the mechanics of identifying members of a district's power structure? The following procedure is suggested. Respected members of the community are asked to identify six to twelve of the most influential citizens in the school district. Or they may be approached with questions such as "Who are the most influential people in the community? If a project were before the community that required a decision by a group of leaders — leaders who nearly everyone would accept — which leaders would be most influential?" Names should be solicited from members of the board of education, and other obvious civic leaders such as the mayor, bank presidents, leading industrialists, the chairman of the Community Chest drive. Lists from these various sources are compared. Those names which appear repeatedly are assumed to make up the community power structure. An additional procedure is to submit the lists of names to a panel of judges made up of respected citizens of long residence in the community. Each judge is asked to rank the names according to influence.

In research conducted at the University of Florida, influential citizens were identified by requesting names from representatives of the following occupations and groups: banking and finance, general business, chamber of commerce, county commissioners, education, farm, general government, news media, and leaders of women's civic organizations. The research indicated that the most reliable sources of nominations included newspaper editors, radio and television executives, and banking and financial executives. Least reliable sources included educators and religious leaders.

Research indicates that influential citizens possess social skills and personality traits which make them more acceptable as leaders. In a study conducted by John Fashett in Valley City, the reasons given for selecting leaders included a persons official position, popularity, and special skills.

The following experience indicates the importance of knowing community structure. The author recalls a problem with a school bus driver who had served the district for many years. He had retired from regular employment but kept the school driving job. The driver regularly attended board of education meetings and always read the board handouts diligently. He was very knowledgeable on school operation. He was a problem, however, for his supervisor because he spread misinformation and rumors among the bus operators which resulted in morale problems among the drivers. The supervisor suggested that his contract not be renewed. At about the same time a study of the community power structure was made which revealed the driver to be an opinion leader among "old line" families. The driver had inherited vast acreage of farm land near a metropolitan area and had considerable wealth and prestige. Needless to say he was not fired. Rather an attempt was made to win him to the side of the school.

INVOLVING REPRESENTATIVES OF THE POWER STRUCTURE

Once the power structure has been identified, representatives of the group must be involved in as many school or school-related projects as possible. In the above example, the superintendent arranged a visit with the driver at his home. He was most appreciative of the visit and was proud to show his newly remodled farm house which centered around a huge wood burning fireplace. The roaring fire provided a relaxing atmosphere to discuss differences. Some of his suggestions were constructive and were put into effect.

Community power leaders should be represented on the school citizens' committee and on ad hoc study groups such as "school finance," "dress code," or "human relations." The author has annually been a part of a "Report on Your Schools Banquet" sponsored by local civic groups in which representatives of the power structure receive a personal invitation.

Prior to deciding on an additional school issue, it is prudent for the superintendent and board to involve the thinking and advice of power structure representatives. Perhaps they can be members of a "blue ribbon" financial study. They should also be a part of the election campaign.

Power leaders need to be nurtured in other ways. The superintendent and board members should occasionally invite them for lunch and allow them to "just talk" about schools and school problems. Such meetings can also be used to obtain their reaction toward future projects or policy changes.

EMPHASIS ON POWER STRUCTURE

As the art of school administration becomes increasingly sophisticated, more attention will be given to the community power structure. Until graduate school programs for administrators offer an "area of concentration" in sociology with emphasis on community structure, the administrator must seek his own self-help. He can attend seminars and conventions which focus on the community and read literature on the subject by William Warner, Robert Lloyd, and August Hollingshead.

A recent publication of the Texas Association of School Boards suggests that schools employ "someone who could identify community organizations and their interests, make an analysis of social groups and their concerns, and learn what values a community holds for its schools."

THE DIFFICULT PUBLICS

Some groups in the community isolate themselves from the mainstream of society and defy all means of communications. Often they do not read newspapers and television viewing is limited to western movies. Many members of such groups have an attitude of "don't bother us." Often such publics exist as a "sub-culture" in a community; the people have their own way of life, vernacular, and value system. Included in such difficult publics are the poor or culturally deprived, ethnic groups, and the wealthy.

Members of the poor and to some extent the ethnic groups, often suspect and resent representatives of the professions and employees of the schools and governmental agencies. They identify school people as part of the establishment which is responsible for their poverty. Unfortunately when they do experience involvement with school employees, it is often over a discipline problem which tends to further reinforce alienation toward school. In other cases such citizens have had bitter experiences with middle class employees or institutional employees such as in police stations, courts, or hospitals. They also refuse to participate in school activities because they feel uncomfortable in the institutionalized school setting, with school employees, and with parents who are active in school affairs.

The author recalls adult classes in basic education (grades 1-6) which were held in a modern elementary school. Class attendance was very irregular. After consulting with representatives of the classes and neighborhood leaders, it was decided to hold class in an old converted factory building. The students felt more comfortable and attendance increased.

Obtaining parent participation in the difficult community is a herculean task which requires an administrator with creative talent, statesmanship, and persistence.

A new elementary school was planned to serve a Cleveland, Ohio, ghetto neighborhood. The parents protested the plan for fear that the new school would promulgate student segregation. The objecting parents vowed that the construction would be bombed and the school would never be built. In the picketing which occurred during construction, one of the protest leaders, a minister, was killed by a bulldozer. In spite of the protest and furor which resulted over the death, the school was built.

Winning over the new community began even before students arrived. Prior to the start of school the principal counseled with her staff — teachers and noncertified — on winning parent support. The principal met with each parent as the children were registered at the new building; each parent was asked to "talk up" the school with friends and neighbors. The Cleveland superintendent of schools set an example: he personally visited the ghetto neighborhood, talked with the parents and listened to their complaints. The chief administrator heard protests that the school was surrounded by a metal fence. Much to the amazement of the protesters, the superintendent had the fence removed.

230

The new school building was safeguarded by neighbors when it was vacant. The principal, accompanied by the building custodian, had visited surrounding homes and asked for help in guarding the building; the citizens responded with enthusiasm.

The school maintained an open-door policy — parents were invited to visit at any time. This policy was promulgated by activities such as:

Students wrote invitations as a classroom exercise.

The administration extended invitations via a weekly news-letter written for parents.

Parent telephone calls always included an invitation from the staff member — "Won't you visit our school?"

Teachers conducted home visits. The principal visited homes to talk with parents often accompanied by the PTA president. A citizens' advisory committee made up of parents and staff members met each month with the principal.

The success of the community effort was indicated by the election results for a school issue voted on a year after the building was opened: the district passed a city-wide bond issue with a 90 percent affirmative vote. At the end of a three-year period there were only six broken windows, and these were broken accidentally.

There are other ways to "involve" parents from the "difficult areas." A portion of the noncertificated personnel can be employed from the difficult neighborhoods as teacher aides, custodians, lay playground supervisors, cafeteria workers. In Berkley, California, parents of children enrolled in the head start program were granted $60.00 scholarships to act as teacher aides for six days of work and to attend 12 parent meetings. In the same city, other parents from difficult areas were hired to assist teachers; the employed parents also visited homes and attempted to develop more positive attitudes toward school.

Employing such personnel provides opportunities for them to become acquainted with school problems and to realize that school employees aren't so bad after all. They also serve as a fountain-head for school information for the hard-to-reach community.

The principal should occasionally leave his desk and visit informally in the difficult neighborhoods. He should request "kaffee klatch" meetings with parents. Such sojourns by the administrator will help him to cultivate friends and enable him to identify potential parent leadership. Parents will also realize that the building principal cares about his parents and students.

The selection of a principal to serve a building which serves a difficult area must be done with care. The administrator must be able to have rapport with the citizens. If the school attendance area contains predominately a single group such as "appalachian migrants," an administrator reared in that area or culture is often more acceptable than a person who is a local product or one who possesses an "ivy league" image. The principal can also increase his effectiveness by living in such a difficult area. Such residence will allow him to become acquainted with the community leadership, better understand the way of life of his citizens, and perhaps be better accepted by the citizens.

Some communities have a large percentange of shift workers. Businesses adjust to such a situation by extending their hours; supermarkets and service stations remain open 24 hours a day. Some schools have a very large group of families where both parents are employed full time. The school must be willing to break with tradition to serve such unique publics. When parent conferences are planned, for example, appointments can be scheduled for the morning hours, the teacher released to return home at 12:00 noon, and conferences again scheduled from 7:00 to 10:00 p.m. As another example, a board of education held two public hearings, one at 1:00 p.m. and another at 8:00 p.m., when it found it necessary to change school attendance lines because of additional new housing and additional student enrollments. Many shift workers who were among those affected by the proposed change would have been unable to attend an evening meeting. Another superintendent who had a high percentage of shift workers in his district, scheduled community meetings on Saturday mornings. This was a day when both parents were at home, and since homes and yards were small, lawn care, even in season, didn't prevent attendance.

A building principal in an economically deprived area increased attendance at PTA meetings by appointing teams of volunteers who visited homes prior to the scheduled event. Each team consisted of a teacher, a parent, and a pupil. When the parents were visited, they were assured that there would be protection for their parked car and their vacant home. If children accompanied parents to the school, they were entertained with film cartoons. Capacity crowds resulted.

Parents in another depressed area were invited to a pre-school orientation. An extensive publicity campaign brought a large turnout: fly-leafs were distributed by children, public health nurses, and religious groups. Additional encouragement and information was provided by the staffs of area medical clinics.

School officials must make greater efforts to work with the poor; a stronger human link with these minority people is needed. To strengthen the link, school people need to become better acquainted with the life styles and the characteristics of low-income people. To improve communications, new and creative approaches needed to reach such people will have to emerge.

The community composed of wealthy, highly educated citizens can be as difficult for the administrator to work with as the depressed area. Because a great number of the adults have been exposed to many years of formal education, they become self-proclaimed experts and critics of the educational program and in the evaluation of teacher performance. The members of one wealthy community were known to boast that they were able to remove at least one incompetent teacher a year from their elementary school. Some jokingly would comment, "Well who are we going to get this year?"

Parents in such neighborhoods often pressure for additions to the school program which "they think" are needed. One parent, for example, organized school mothers to persuade school officials to have an organized exercise program for students over the noon hour so that the children wouldn't "waste their time in play." Mothers in such districts have time, energy, and talent which they may be willing to share with the school staff, but these must be channeled into positive and purposeful projects. Occasionally the administrator must "draw the line" when parents become involved or make decisions in areas which have to be reserved for the professional educator.

CITIZEN VOLUNTEERS IN THE SCHOOL

Increasingly citizens are being used in the school and in the classrooms as "volunteers." Such service helps to build bridges between the school and the community. Parents have long stood at the fringes, at the threshold of education, as PTA participants and room mothers. Now more and more they are serving as human resources for the classrooms. The schools and children benefit because:

More talent is available for teaching students.

The school and community work together in a joint effort to teach students.

Citizens learn about the goals, objectives, and achievements of their schools.

In a Portland, Oregon school, eighth graders canvassed their neighborhood to distribute a questionnaire for citizens to indicate specialties which they would share at school. In White Plains, New York, several hundred parent volunteers are used to supplement the classroom teachers. In other districts, TV weathermen, photographers, or any area resident with an occupation or experience that would interest high schoolers is frequently called in for Curriculum Days or Career Days.

COOPERATION WITH OTHER COMMUNITY ORGANIZATIONS

The operation of the public schools is in competition with other civic, social, and governmental agencies for funds, community support, and recognition. These groups must work together, however, for maximum effect. Cooperation can be increased by a representative of one organization working occasionally with a competing group. For example, a school administrator can serve on the "community planning commission." Minutes of meetings can be exchanged between organizations such as the school, city council, county commissioners. Occasionally a joint meeting of officers of the board of education, city government, and county government, to exchange long-range goals, will result in improved understanding and cooperation. Such organizations cannot afford to live in isolation of one another.

THE COMMUNITY AS A STUDENT LABORATORY

The school must extend its curriculum and learning resources into the community and use the community as a learning laboratory. Several schools have been recently established without the traditional school

234

building. Students are taught in museums, art institutes, government buildings, and industrial plants which exist in the district.

Students can make increased use of the community in other ways. Pupils can survey citizens on problems of current issue: pollution, zoning, recreation, public transportation. Occasionally results from such studies motivate citizens and government officials into action and if so, the bonds between the school and the community are greatly strengthened. Student volunteers work in social agencies and as a result discover community needs in areas of health, welfare, recreation, and home life. School musical groups perform in hospitals, nursing homes, and detention homes. Students sponsor community service projects which may include (1) cleaning up an abandoned lot to develop a play area; (2) tree plantings; (3) constructive projects at Halloween.

The school curriculum is extended to the community when work experience programs, such as distributive education and a secretarial co-op program are offered by the school. Such programs allow school employees and students to meet and work with members of the community and make for better understanding and communication.

School staffs need to be familiar with community resources. A "community resources guide" should be available for each teacher which identifies businesses, industries, or social agencies; addresses, phone numbers, persons to contact. Administrators need to encourage maximum use of community resources: fire stations, water department, power company, incinerators, police stations, bakeries, auto industries, publishing companies, steel plants, and other industries.

One teachers' association got different organizations such as a government space agency and a greeting card company to offer attractive field trips for teachers to sell them on the value of field trips for students.

SCHOOL BUILDINGS FOR COMMUNITY USE

New schools which are being planned or schools which are to be remodeled should be designed for community use. School buildings can be fully utilized only if they are used by both students and adults. Maximum adult use requires increased parking areas. Building facilities which are used by students and adults need to be grouped together: community room, gymnasium, shops, art rooms, foreign language rooms, and cafeteria. Adults require greater storage areas for projects. The Flint, Michigan, schools are nationally known for an effective "community-school program."

As work weeks shorten and workers retire earlier, adults have more and more time and desire to pursue interests in greater depth through adult education courses. The writer had his assistant superintendent in charge of adult education welcome all adult students the first night of each session. This builds rapport with a new group of voters often, for many of the students no longer have pupils in school.

Imagine a board of education room being used for an Alcoholics Anonymous meeting on Sunday nights. It was easier to open this building for one group than a school building. The AA members, a zealous lot anyway, support school issues. Such subtle sells are necessary in this age of bond-issue-resident voters.

CHAPTER XV

PUBLIC RELATIONS AND COMMUNICATIONS DURING TEACHER NEGOTIATIONS

PUBLIC RELATIONS AND COMMUNICATIONS DURING TEACHER NEGOTIATIONS

The following chapter describes public relations and communications techniques which can be used during the teacher negotiation process. It is not the purpose of this section to explain the mechanics of negotiations; such information will be supplied only as necessary to explain the communications techniques which are presented.

SOME BASIC PRINCIPLES OF NEGOTIATIONS

Since 1961, when New York City became the first major school district to agree to collective bargaining, there has been an avalanche of school districts which signed negotiations agreements; a new era of board-staff relationships resulted. Many boards of education were ill prepared for the negotiations battles which they encountered; many board negotiators "gave away the store" when threatened with teacher walkouts. Since those beginning years, however, both board and teacher negotiators have become increasingly sophisticated and adept. In many districts, the negotiations process seems to work well for school employees; boards have learned to live with and accept the process.

The following factors, according to teachers and their leadership, have led to increased teacher demands and militancy:

Inadequate salaries
High pupil-teacher class sizes
Lack of meaningful involvement in school operation
Poor human relations when dealing with the staff
Inadequate supplies and facilities.

Whether individual citizens agree with these factors or not is not significant. The teachers and their leaders feel this way and they are determined to improve their lot.

The following basic principles of negotiations are presented; the public relations and communications techniques which follow are based on these principles.

> The superintendent of schools should not serve as the negotiating team spokesman; preferably, he shouldn't even serve on the team. An assistant or a professional negotiator should represent the board and superintendent.

> The board members must not become involved in the negotiations process. Their contribution should be limited to establishing guidelines for the negotiating team. Board members lack the necessary time, patience and expertise required for negotiating.

Having the board and superintendent removed from the negotiating table provides the board team with resilience: if the team errors in judgment, the agreement does not have to be approved by the superintendent or the board.

The person who is selected as chief negotiator must have a position of trust; he must have the full confidence of the superintendent and the leeway to be flexible within agreed-upon limits; he must have access to the superintendent for information, advice and direction. The members of the board's negotiating team must be encouraged to attend seminars and training programs in order to keep informed of current negotiating techniques and skills.

PUBLIC RELATIONS AND THE NEGOTIATIONS AGREEMENT

The development of a negotiations agreement, sometimes referred to as a "master agreement," is an important part of agreeing to staff negotiations. Such a document spells out the basic negotiations procedures and ground rules. Typical agreements include philosophy, recognition, procedures, impasse, grievance, amendments and span of agreement. Legal assistance should be employed in the development of this most important document since its contents will usually affect the negotiating process for many years. A well-prepared agreement can help both, staff and board representatives; it can provide the vehicle for an orderly resolution of problems before they cause complications.

After a negotiations agreement is adopted by the board of education, the teaching staff will typically make its own interpretation of the instrument's meaning; the administration and board members will do the same. The interpretations reflect the biased opinions of the respective groups and are different and often in conflict. Although difficult to accomplish, an interpretation fair to both groups is needed. This may be possible by establishing a joint teacher association — administration committee which would agree on interpretations acceptable to both groups. Legal advice would be needed because a legal interpretation of a clause is often completely different from that of a layman. The committee could publish its results or members could meet with the staff of each school to explain the document and answer questions.

In the absence of the joint effort described above, building principals need to be given a thorough explanation of the document so they can interpret the agreement to their staffs. If the explanations are too administratively oriented, the teachers' association will ask for time to give its own interpretation to the staff.

THE NEGOTIATING TEAM

Negotiating teams are most often limited to 3-5 members. If the team exceeds five, it can become unwieldly; the time consumed in deliberations and discussions becomes prohibitive. Also, the chances of a breach in secrecy increases when a larger number is involved. A member of the board's team is usually selected because of a specialty: finance, law, personnel.

241

The board's team spokesman must be able to think quickly, be articulate, remain firm but polite and courteous. No one should speak at the table but the chief negotiator. Other team members communicate to him by writing notes or by requesting a caucus.

The chief spokesman should insist that all questions be directed to him. Team members should never reply to questions or volunteer information unless requested by the team spokesman. The cheif negotiator may, at his descretion, call upon members of the team to speak to a topic. Team members must guard against revealing their feelings or positions on a topic by facial expressions.

During the negotiations session, any member of the team should have the right to request a caucus. The request should be signaled to the chief spokesman; in most cases such a request should be honored by the spokesman.

THE ROLE OF THE PRINCIPAL DURING NEGOTIATIONS

Until recently, the building principal was largely ignored in the negotiating process. He was not wanted as a member of the teachers' team and was not given a position on the board's team. Often, during negotiations, the staff knew more about progress results than the building principal. Increasing numbers of principals are now recognized as part of the management team and serve as board representatives on the negotiating team.

The increased number of strikes has propelled the principal to be recognized as a member of the management team. When strikes occur, boards usually insist that the buildings remain open for instruction. This requires the principal to be in his building and to conduct school with nonstriking teachers, paraprofessionals and supervisory help. Prior to strike action, principals and supervisors are usually reminded that they are expected to support the board's position; nonsupport, they are cautioned, will lead to nonrenewal of contracts.

Increasingly, principals are serving on the boards' negotiating teams. They do not act as chief spokesmen, but are available to advise on matters which affect principals and building operations. Experience on the negotiating team helps principals to better understand the mechanics, complexities and frustrations of the process; they are able to keep other principals informed and principals are better able to fulfill their roles as management team members.

The superintendent should provide confidential briefings for all of the principals as the negotiations proceed. He should provide for discussion and feedback, particularly on items affecting their aspect of the operation. This feedback can be a valuable source of ideas which can be utilized by the board of education's negotiating team.

There are times when a building principal must represent the board and interpret news related to negotiations to his staff:

> An election to determine the "representative group" has been requested. The election and the necessary ground rules must be explained to the staff. The principal must represent the board to insure correct implementation of the election procedure; staff questions must be answered.

> During an impasse, the principal must interpret and defend the board's position.

> If a strike or slowdown should occur, the principal must explain the illegal aspects of the act and the consequences of the action.

When an agreement is finally reached, each principal should be so informed immediately; such news should not be obtained from faculty members. At a later time, the principal must have a complete explanation of the new agreement. Occasionally, when clauses are difficult to explain, role-playing can complement verbal descriptions. For example, the following scenario can be acted out for a newly adopted personal leave policy:

> A high school mathematics teacher who wishes to receive full salary while visiting his wife's dying uncle has not received a satisfactory answer (for him) from the building representative, the department chairman, or the principal at the informal procedure level. As a result, he plans to file a grievance against the principal.

NEGOTIATIONS AND OTHER ADMINISTRATIVE GROUPS

Another group which is often overlooked in the negotiations is the central office professional staff including the educational support

get angry and fight back when intemperate accusations are made or when 'the straw that broke the camel's back' is hurled on the table.

2. Avoid 'off the record' comments. Actually, nothing is 'off the record.' Innocently made remarks have a way of coming back to haunt their author. Be careful to say only what you are willing to have quoted.

3. Don't be overcandid. Inexperienced negotiators may, with the best of intentions, desire to 'lay the cards on the table face up.' This may be done in the mistaken notion that everybody fully understands the other and utter frankness is desired. Complete candor doesn't always serve the best interests of productive negotiation. . . .

4. Be long on listening. Usually a good listener makes a good negotiator. It is wise to let your 'adversaries' do the talking — at least in the beginning.

5. Don't be afraid of a 'little heat.' Discussions sometimes generate quite a bit of 'heat.' Don't be afraid of it. It never hurts to let the 'opposition' sound off even when you may be tempted to hit back.

6. Watch the voice level. A wise practice is to keep the pitch of the voice down even though the temptation may be strong to let it rise under the excitement of emotional stress.

7. Refrain from a flat 'no.' Especially in the earlier stages of negotiation it is best to avoid giving a flat 'no' answer to a proposition. It doesn't help to work yourself into a box by being totally negative 'too early in the game.'

8. Respect your adversary. Respect those who are seated on the opposite side of the table. Assume that their motives are as sincere as your own, at least until proven otherwise.

9. Be patient. If necessary, be willing to sit out tiresome tirades. Time has a way of being on the side of the patient negotiator.

10. Avoid waving 'red flags.' There are some statements that irritate teachers and merely heighten their antipathies. Find out what these are and avoid their use. Needless waving of 'red flags' only infuriates."

NEWS RELEASES

During the beginning stages of negotiations, agreement should be sought on the release of information during the negotiating process. Sometimes the two teams can agree that news given out will be in the form of joint releases. It is customary and desirable for neither side to issue progress reports during negotiations. If the sessions become militant or bitter, however, one side or another will occasionally make a unilateral news release. It will be a biased statement favoring the group which issues the information. This, in turn, forces the other side to make a statement, also usually biased. If a board is forced to make a rebuttal statement, it is often made directly to the staff; in addition, it may be made to the news media. In the past, board representatives have been reluctant to "fight back" when teachers have taken to the media. There has been a feeling of "let's keep it on a high plane." Silence in such cases plays into the hands of the teachers; the board must on certain occasions make public statements on its positions.

AN AGENDA

It is desirable to have an agenda distributed in advance of any negotiations session. A representative from each group can meet in advance to prepare the agenda. A list of topics to be covered allows team members to prepare in advance of the meeting; it lessens the danger of getting off the subject. Once an agenda is established, it should be agreed that no other items are to be added.

THE WALKOUT DURING A NEGOTIATING SESSION

Occasionally, as a result of an impasse or an exchange of insults, one party in negotiations will walk out. A board team should avoid such a tactic. In the eyes of the teachers and community, the party which walks out is indicating militancy and insincerity; public relations-wise, the team will be hurt.

DEVELOPING AGREEMENTS

When the two teams reach agreement on various clauses, both spokesmen usually initial the final wording agreed upon. Some negotiators perfer to not initiate such agreements but give only verbal approval. This allows them the flexibility of withdrawal in favor of other concessions as the negotiations proceed.

The final agreement will have to be studied and understood by both the board and teaching staff prior to final ratification. The wording, therefore, should be straight forward and void of ambiguities. The exact procedure for releasing the contents to the news media and public should be agreed upon by both parties.

The principal of each building is the key person to the successful implementation of a new contract: he is needed to explain the contents of the agreement to his staff. If a principal does not successfully fulfill this role, a vacuum will develop. The teachers' association representatives will then move in to provide an association interpretation of the contract. The central office staff must move quickly after ratification to arm principals with the necessary information to explain the pact to the staff.

DURING A CRISIS PERIOD

Experienced negotiators realize that the negotiating process occasionally goes through periods of crisis; impasse threatens; a strike vote occurs; a strike takes place. It is best during a crisis to have one person serve as a spokesman for the board and administration. This person is usually the superintendent, an assistant superintendent or the public relations person. During such difficult times, unusual communications problems may arise. For example, the teachers' group may release incorrect information concerning the board's final salary offer. In this case, a communication from the superintendent or board to all staff members must carry the actual facts.

When an impasse is reached, it is often to the board's advantage to make its final offer known to the staff and community. Silence, although comfortable, may be an advantage to the teachers' team. Besides, if the board's position is fair and reasonable, release of the final offer may result in community support.

Several suggestions to gain public support for the board's position are presented by Richard Neal in *Avoiding and Controlling Teacher Strikes,* Educational Service Bureau, Inc., 1835 K. Street, N. W., Washington, D.C. 20006.

"1. All public statements chastising the teachers should refer to the teachers' union (or 'association'). Every effort should be made to avoid radicalizing the individual teacher. . . . The board should word its releases to show that the association or the union has been responsible for the damage to the schools.

2. The local power structure should be contacted by the school board and its. . . administrators to enlist . . . support for the board. Quite often the owners of the local newspaper are more helpful than the editors.

3. The PTA's should be contacted. . . the board's position should be made clear. . . .

4. Keep in daily touch with the media. The board's spokesman should always be available. The public deserves to hear from its elected representatives."

Teachers will occasionally resort to paid advertising in support of their position at the bargaining table. Again, a board will have to counteract with a description of its own position. The news media will normally carry a rebuttal as a news story and a paid retort will not be necessary.

If a "hotline telephone" has not previously been in operation, such a phone service might be a valuable tool at least for the duration of the crisis. The public relations director is usually responsible for a hotline operation. In a small district the superintendent may have to delegate the responsibility to a building administrator or competent secretary. There will be many citizen questions which can be effectively handled by a hotline operation. Typical questions are "Is there a strike on?"; "When will school reopen?"; "Are teachers paid for strike days?"; "What was the board's last offer?"

During periods of militancy, administrators and board members must often carry the label of "black hats." Criticism is heaped on one or several school officials for the board's stand. Caustic accusations are made verbally, through teacher newsletters or through the news media. For example, one faculty was at impasse. When attending a September orientation program, the teachers stood up and turned their backs to the superintendent and board president when they addressed the audience. Individuals involved in negotiations must realize that accusations and insults must occasionally be part of the process; such actions cannot be taken as a personal affront.

During a crisis period, staff members may air their demands before classroom students in an attempt to seek pupil and parent support for their demands. Many parents resent such teacher tactics as indicated in a parent poll which was conducted by a secondary school parent organization following a teachers' walkout. The question asked of parents was:

Do you feel that your children have been influenced in the classroom by the negotiation problems between the teaching staff and the school administration? Yes   No   If the answer is "yes" please explain how they have been influenced:

Replies: Teachers talked freely in the class of their views of planned walkout — 15; the teacher walkout had a bad effect on children as they lost respect for teachers — 4; children sensed disagreement and did not like to see it — 2; children ask questions so should be given answers by teachers — 1; child was too young to understand — 1.

Use of the above-described tactic results in a loss of community support and respect for the teachers' cause. Leaders of the association and staff members, themselves, however, are the people who will have to act to correct such abuse.

PREPARING FOR THE STRIKE

If indications of militancy occur in the district prior to or during negotiations, the administration should develop a "strike plan." The strike plan describes the responsibilities of administrators and supervisors during a walk-out. In most work stoppages, the boards of education keep the schools open with nonstriking personnel. Such plans describe techniques to operate school with minimum staff; activities are listed which can be conducted in large groups.

When such a plan has been developed, it should not remain secretive. Faculty members should be aware that such a plan has been distributed; news of its existence can be disseminated discretely by the administrative staff. The following items related to communications are found in such strike plans:

All information and answers to questions will be handled through the superintendent's office.

A meeting will be held daily, after school hours for all school administrators.

Volunteer parental help will not be solicited. "Walk in" volunteers, however, will be utilized.

Parental information plan: PTA room mothers will notify parents in case of early dismissal or other emergency.

Someone will be designated at each school building to handle incoming calls.

The superintendent will be provided with an alternate telephone number, such as a resident living next door to the school — in case telephone lines are jammed or cut.

A camera and film should be available at each building.

A bull horn or portable public address system should be available at each building.

In the event the news media come directly to a building, they should be asked to call the superintendent and seek permission to interview and film. If the superintendent refuses permission, ask them to leave.

As an additional precaution, alternate unlisted telephone numbers should be identified for the central office. Because of the possibility of telephone jamming, it may also be desirable to install an extra unlisted telephone line to each high school building.

HARASSMENT TACTICS

A local association or union can harass a board by calling for an investigation of the school operation by an outside evaluating team appointed by the state teachers' organization. Such investigation reports usually cite shortcomings in the school operation to make the board and administrators appear inadequate. Although boards will sometimes cooperate in such a study, the results are usually biased and not of objective value.

The teachers' team may attempt to "wear down" a board's negotiating team through long sessions or through other harassment techniques. The plan is to physically and emotionally wear out the opposition which will lead to capitulation at the negotiating table. In one district, for example, representatives of the teaching staff brought campers to the board parking lot to allow for prolonged sessions. Loud speakers blared which kept the pickets charged and announced negotiation progress reports. Board teams cannot allow such tactics and should insist on a recess when fatigue results after long sessions. Negotiators should not make important decisions when fatigued.

Occasionally, the teachers will present their positions through leaflets handcarried to every house in the district. The association may establish an "information center" in a convenient location; a "hot line" telephone number may be advertised and citizens encouraged to telephone for the "facts." Officers of the association may use the "letters to the editors" section of the local newspaper.

THE STRIKE

When all attempts to negotiate a settlement fail and a strike is declared, the board must present its final position to the staff and public: the final salary offer and remaining unresolved problems. This information can be released in a special newsletter made available to the staff and mailed to each resident in the school district. The information can be released through the news media. The PTA's and citizens' committees can also disseminate the board's position. Both techniques can be used. Too often, after negotiations fail, the community hears only of the teachers' position.

During a strike, boards of education usually keep school buildings open and operating with the help of supervisors and nonstriking teachers and paraprofessionals. Keeping schools open provides a penalty (loss of pay) for those who strike. The policy of staying open with salary deductions for strikers should be made known, in writing, to all staff members prior to the walkout. The leaders should also be informed that strike days will not be made up. The following statement appeared in a letter to staff members from a superintendent prior to a staff walkout:

"Pay will be deducted for days absent for work stoppage; additional days will not be added to the calendar year in order to make up such days."

In states where a strike is illegal, the memorandum should emphasize that a work stoppage is an illegal action.

A strike headquarters is usually established at the central office. It serves as the communications center. There should be only one spokesman for the board during the crisis; in small districts this will be the superintendent; in larger systems the spokesman is usually the district's information officer or an assistant superintendent. Board members and other administrators should be instructed to not make comments about the strike.

The spokesman should be identified for the news media. The news representatives should also be told that any statements made by other school officials are unofficial.

No personal attacks on anyone should be made by the board members or administrative personnel at any time.

During the strike, the teachers' team may attempt to by-pass the board's team and request a separate meeting with the board or board president. It is most important that the Board members refuse such overtures; the teachers cannot be allowed to by-pass the negotiating table; the process must be played according to the rules.

The board should never agree during a strike to a public meeting to air impasse problems.

AFTER THE STRIKE

A staff strike results in much bitterness among employees. Prior to the strike there is conflict among staff members as to the ethics and legality of the strike procedure. During and after the strike, antagonism develops between those who strike and those who refuse to do so. In schools which have experienced a strike, some staff members still refuse to talk to one another a year following the event. In one school, a teacher who remained on duty was asked to leave his car pool and find another way to get to school.

A hugh public relations task remains following a strike. School officials can only pick up the pieces and attempt to rebuild faculty relations and staff - administration-board relations.

Community anxiety, pressure and backlash occur during during and after the strike. If the buildings are kept open during the walkout (usually with skeletal staffs), a segment of the population, especially those supportive of the teachers, will criticize school officials for operating schools with less than a full staff; they maintain that students are in danger because of inadequate supervision. But, if the board closes the schools, as a result of a strike, criticism results from another segment because students are not in school and roam the community; they are without proper supervision. If schools are closed, school officials may also be accused of a "lock out" because some teachers would prefer to work. The board can only determine its policy and then hold to it, regardless of criticism.

CITIZEN VOLUNTEERS DURING A STRIKE

Some school officials have solicited citizen volunteers to staff classrooms during a strike. Sometimes, PTA's have been asked to organize volunteers to man classrooms. The recruitment of citizen volunteers during a strike is not recommended. The volunteers are labeled as strike breakers by the teachers and results in a bitter conflict between staff and citizens. The school cannot afford to have teacher — parent relationships destroyed as a result of the strike. Those citizens, however, who come to a school on their own to volunteer, can be used, and criticism will be minimal.

USE OF SCHOOL COMMUNICATIONS FACILITIES

School officials usually allow the teachers' association the use of the school courier, staff mailboxes and bulletin board space. Guidelines should be established, however, to avoid abuse of these facilities. The name of the person responsible for a teacher publication should be required on all documents; the building principal should receive a copy of the material before it is posted or distributed.

USE OF STAFF NEWSLETTER DURING NEGOTIATIONS

Many schools publish a periodic staff newsletter. This vehicle would be convenient to use to carry administrative interpretations and news during problem times faced in negotiations. The staff newsletter, however, should not be used as a vehicle to disseminate news related to negotiations; this would detract from the newsletter which is designed to carry objective news about the over-all school operation. The administration should, rather, communicate through a special memo or newsletter.

APPENDIX A

JOB DESCRIPTION

LOS ANGELES, CALIFORNIA
Supervisor of Public Information

1. Interprets information and actions orginating with the board of education, the superintendent, and the staff; coordinates and supervises the dissemination of such information through the media of radio, television, and the press.

2. Serves as spokesman for the board of education and the administrative staff relating to school system policy, educational philosophy, and administrative procedures.

3. Serves as a member of the Superintendent's Legislative Committee, the Ethnicity Committee, and as a representative on the Division Heads Council.

4. Cooperates, upon request of division heads, in evaluating and interpreting educational information concerning the operating divisions of the district, and coordinates and supervises its release through the administrative and supervisory personnel of such divisions.

5. Develops a positive and continuing program of reporting so as to keep the public aware of the services being rendered and the problems being solved by the district.

6. Serves as an advisor to review and make suggestions related to public relations aspects of anticipated or planned TV, radio, or film programs.

7. Supervises a service which provides constant information about school calendars, school locations and boundaries; plans coordinated public information programs for various activities of the district so that information released is accurate and appropriately timed with regard to public relations.

8. Provides in-service education to teacher, administrative, and other personnel in methods and techniques of selection, organization, and dissemination of educational information.

9. In emergencies, is immediately available to receive and assess information regarding the situation, advises the superintendent or his designated representative regarding the situation, and takes whatever steps are deemed necessary, based on the severity of the situation, to receive from and dispense information to members of the district staff and the public.

10. Assists in the evaluation of the educational significance of special activities and contests.

11. Serves as an official representative of the administrative staff of the Los Angeles City Schools at certificated conventions and professional organizations; supervises the planning, makes necessary arrangements, and assists in conducting state-wide and nation-wide conventions and conferences held locally for which the district acts as host.

12. Assists administrators and teachers in the solution of local community relations problems at individual schools.

13. Arranges and conducts meetings for interpretation of the educational philosophy, policies, and administrative procedures of the board of education to interested public groups such as the Parent-Teachers Association, Coordinating Councils, and community business, labor, and professional groups.

14. Performs other duties as assigned.

APPENDIX B

STAFF NEWSLETTER

Events

BEREA
CITY
SCHOOL
DISTRICT
Berea, Ohio

**FROM THE
SUPERINTENDENT'S OFFICE**

Position Available

There is a Unit Coordinator position available at Roehm Junior High School. Anyone interested in being considered for the position should send written no- tification to Dr. Somerville by Friday, June 8. Interviews will be arranged as soon as possible.

**Committee Plans
Social Studies
Activities**

Social studies articulation meetings have resulted in plans for a number of ve- hicles designed to reestablish communication among building social studies departments and individuals within departments. A steering committee com- posed of Gary Croy (Berea), Larry Pilarski (Midpark), Fred Parsh (Ford), Jay Gradisher (Roehm), Ed Mennell and Gary Puntel (Middleburg), and Jim Langer has agreed to act on the following ideas during the   school year:

(1) Publish a regularly scheduled social science newsletter. Newsletters will feature school or program changes, materials exchange, personal- ity features, calendar of social studies activities, and meetings and research findings.

(2) Specific orientation programs for new social studies teachers.

(3) Regular meetings of the social studies leadership group.

(4) Development of workshops for the sharing of skills and techniques among staff members; utilization of out-of-system consultants for upgrading skills and attaining in-depth information related to social studies con- cepts.

The steering committee is also considering informal get-togethers, topical dis- cussions and visitations as possible ways "to get social studies staff members to- gether and learn about one another as human beings."

**Construction Will
Begin On New
Hospital**

The Board of Trustees of the Southwest Health Care Center extend an invitation to all staff members to attend ground-breaking ceremonies for the new hospital facility on June 21 at 2:00 p.m.

Vale Elected

Dick Vale, Ford Junior High principal, has been voted   President-Elect of the Ohio Association of Secondary School Principals. Congratulations, Dick!

**Can Schools Be
Sued For Failing
To Teach?**

Can the schools be held legally responsible if a child fails to learn to read and write at an adult level? This is a major issue in a California court case involv- ing an unidentified pupil named "Peter Doe" and the San Francisco Unified School District. At issue is whether Peter Doe can claim $1 million in damages for having been graduated from high school with the ability to read only at a fifth-grade level. The child's mother also claims that school officials defrauded her by repeatedly assuring her that Peter was progressing normally in school.

The suit contends that under California law the state is responsible for minimum educational standards and establishing a system to turn out a student with these skills.

CALENDAR

Monday, June 4	8:30 a.m.	Administrative Council Meeting – Staff Room 1
	9:00 a.m.	Cafeteria Meeting – Curriculum Library
	7:30 p.m.	PTA Council Handbook Workshop – Staff Room 1
Wednesday, June 6	8:15 a.m.	Instructional Consultants' Meeting – Curriculum Library
	2:15 p.m.	Head Custodians' Meeting – Staff Room 1
Thursday, June 7	ALL DAY	MAKO – Curriculum Library

HAVE A GREAT SUMMER!

School's out, School's out,
No more Principals,
No more Grade Books,
No more Students' Dirty Looks!

APPENDIX C

SCHOOL BOARD REPORT

Board Report

| Berea Board of Education | BEREA – BROOK PARK – MIDDLEBURG HEIGHTS |

Administrative
Appointments
Approved

John H. Evans, presently an assistant superintendent in the Rocky River system, was appointed principal of Gallaher School. Mr. Evans has 15 years experience as an elementary and middle school principal in Pennsylvania, New Jersey, and Ohio.

David Minich was named Assistant Principal at Berea High School. He is now a Unit Coordinator at the school.

William Hansen, who is now a guidance assistant at Brookpark Memorial School, has been assigned as a cadet principal for the   school year.

Retirees Honored

The Board of Education honored 14 staff members who are retiring after many years of service to the young people of our school communities:

Mr. Clyde Boone	– Supervisor of Maintenance
Mrs. Violet Boone	– Gallaher School Principal
Mrs. Mary Dunfee	– Lechner School Second-Grade Teacher
Mrs. Irene Eshmont	– Roehm Junior High Cafeteria Manager
Mrs. Helen Gardner	– Lechner School Cafeteria Manager
Miss Martha Jackman	– Fairwood School Fifth-Grade Teacher
Mrs. Sarah Marshall	– Roehm Junior High Librarian
Mr. Bernard McKenzie	– Central School Head Custodian
Mr. Theodore Priver	– Gallaher School Head Custodian
Mrs. Dorotha Robinson	– Berea High School Latin and History Teacher
Mr. Fred Schwandt	– Middlebrook School Head Custodian
Miss Christine West	– Berea High School English Teacher
Mrs. Lydia Williams	– Roehm Junior High School Counselor
Mrs. Geraldine Winsper	– Ford Junior High School English Teacher

Central School
Will Become
Supplementary
Center

As a result of Board action, Central Elementary School will be used as a Supplementary Education Center for school and community educational services. The Adult, Vocational, and Summer School departments will occupy the building beginning in July of this year. Adult Basic Education classes, evening high school classes and many of the non-credit, apprentice, and technical division classes will also be located at the building.

Other community oriented programs such as an expanded day school adult education program and daytime adult recreational activities are being considered. The Central building will also provide a place for developing and piloting innovative and alternative education programs.

Budget Hearing
Will Be Held

The General Code of Ohio stipulates that boards of education adopt a budget for the fiscal year and that this budget must be submitted to the county auditor by July 20.

Copies of the budget are filed with the clerk of the board of education and will be available for inspection for at least ten days prior to adoption.

Staff Appointed For
Reading Program

The Board approved the appointment of staff for the Summer Remedial Reading Project which is funded by the Federal Government. The project affects 100 children in grades two through five and is operated under the Elementary and Secondary Education Act of 1965.

Newsletter
Information
Questioned

Mrs. Luff reacted to a paragraph in the latest edition of Your Schools by stating that she was pleased that Berea High band members who went on the Mexico trip had a successful experience. However, she indicated her disappointment that the trip was mentioned in the newsletter since Board members did not consider the trip part of the school program.

Athletic Director
Honored

Dr. Mayer presented a plaque to athletic director, Robert Purdy. Bob received the award for outstanding service from the National Council for Secondary School Athletic Directors.

Superintendent
Takes New
Position

Dr. Mayer announced that he would be leaving on or about July 1st to accept a position as superintendent of the Roseville, Michigan schools. He thanked members of the community for the support they have given during his four year tenure in Berea.

Board members thanked Dr. Mayer for his contributions to the school system and wished him well in his new assignment.

Since the Roseville Board of Education will not act officially on the Superintendent's contract until Wednesday, the Berea Board of Education will meet in an adjourned session on Thursday morning, June 14, at 8:30 a.m. to officially accept Dr. Mayer's resignation.

Board Acts On
Personnel Items

In other action Board members:

(1) appointed a new Supervisor of Transportation. Albert G. Cook was awarded a two-year contract to succeed Wilson Leatherman who will retire at the end of the present calendar year.

(2) approved a change in the Special Merit Award policy which will increase the stipend from $100 to $200 for staff members who have made outstanding contributions under the criteria listed in the policy.

(3) employed 12 secondary school instructors, 12 elementary instructors, and six driver education teachers for various summer school programs.

TY:hb

INTRA-STAFF COMMUNICATION

APPENDIX E

BOARD — SUPERINTENDENT GUIDELINES

The Superintendent presented the following guidelines for Board-Superintendent working relations; they are considered necessary if the Superintendent is to function effectively:

1. ### Administration vs. Policy

   The Board of Education establishes policies — what it wants done; the Administration carries out that policy. For example, the Board may have a policy which states that "students who must travel through hazardous traffic conditions to get to school shall have bus transportation." It is the administrator who carries this policy out and determines when conditions are sufficiently hazardous to justify bussing.

   There are some gray areas where policy-making and Administration may overlap. In these areas we must work together.

2. ### Staff Reports to Board of Education

   All staff reports to the Board of Education are asked to be sent through the Superintendent. Staff members are not to contact the Board Members individually without informing the Superintendent.

3. ### Board Members and Contacting Staff Members

   Board Members are asked not to contact staff members directly; they should be contacted through the Superintendent. For example, if a Board Member has a criticism of a teacher or principal, this should be presented to the Superintendent - never to that person directly. If a Board Member has a suggestion on how to improve a school, it should go to the Superintendent who should evaluate the proposal, and if worthy implement. By going through the Superintendent, he is able to be informed; also a principal may feel pressured or obligated if presented by a Board Member; the Superintendent can avoid having a principal called by several Board Members on the same problem. If the Board Member does contact a staff member, I request that you ask that staff member to inform me of the contact.

4. ### Ideas for New Programs or Program Changes

   Board Members who have suggestions for new programs or program changes are asked to present them to the Superintendent. The reasons for going through the Superintendent are the same as those above. The Superintendent must evaluate the proposal, anyway.

5. ### Complaints Received by Board Members

   a). A parent calls to complain about a student being given an unfair grade. . .

   Recommended Board Procedure:

   Ask parent to discuss the problem with the teacher or principal.

263

b). A parent calls to complain about a teacher...

Recommended Board Procedure:

Ask parent to discuss the problem with the teacher or principal.

c). A parent calls to complain about a principal...

Recommended Board Procedure:

Ask the parent to arrange a conference with the principal.

If the parent isn't satisfied with the conference in a, b, c, he or she should contact the next highest official.

If parents refuse to talk to the teacher or principal, suggest they talk to the Assistant Superintendent; if still not satisfied, to talk with the Superintendent.

A Board Member should not conduct an investigation on his own.

6. Board Voting

Although a unanimous vote is desirable, the Superintendent doesn't expect a unanimous vote on every issue. Differences as much as possible, however, should be discussed in work sessions.

7. Negotiations

Guidelines for the negotiations process should be given by the Board of Education. The negotiating team is expected to settle within these guidelines. Board Members should not enter the negotiation process. The staff would like to get to Board Members since they have the power and the final say. We should make every effort to avoid that trap.

APPENDIX F

PARENT NEWSLETTER

C. A. Thomas School

NEWSLETTER

ANN DODDRIDGE   16699 E. BAGLEY ROAD   BEREA CITY SCHOOL DISTRICT

PRINCIPAL   MIDDLEBURG HEIGHTS, 44130   234-8610

SPELLING CHAMP   Congratulations to Kathy Kuhn, sixth grade, who won the C. A. Thomas Spelling Contest on Wednesday and Jennifer Gericke, fifth grade, who was runner-up.

THOMAS FAIR WINNERS   The lucky winners of the stuffed animals at the Thomas Fair were: Susan Dittebrand, Scott Beier, Diane Frampton, Judy Dibble, Jennifer Harmon, Sherianne Steinbach, Holly Wirth, Rodney Geschke, Dave Felts, and Barbara Hart.

SALAD LUNCHEON   Have you remembered to send in your reservation for the PTA Salad Luncheon to be held on Wednesday, May 9th, at 12:00 Noon? This is one of the highlights of the year with good food, installation of officers and an outstanding speaker, Neriman Mehmet, A.F.S. student from Cyprus. You are reminded to bring your choice of salad or dessert plus table service. Baby sitting will be provided by Sixth Grade girls. Please be sure children had lunch before coming. For reservations call Mrs. Nebesar-234-9928, Mrs. Wirth-243-4471 or Mrs.Stochl-234-6803.

ARBOR DAY   Arbor Day was celebrated at Thomas School today. The Student Coucil President, Tom Hronek, made a presentation on Arbor Day and the Council representative from each class planted a tree.

FIELD TRIP   On Monday the third grades took a boat trip on the Cuyahoga River viewing industry, types of bridges and problems of pollution. Roommothers, Mrs. Robert Davies, Mrs. Robert Richmond, and Mrs. Raymond Ebner accompanied the classes.

CAMP MI-BRO-BE   Miss DeMitchell's Sixth Grade Class will spend next week at Camp Mi-Bro-Be experiencing out-door education and making many new friends from other schools within our district.

LIBRARIANS VISIT   On Monday and Wednesday, May 7 and 9, the Middleburg Heights Librarians, Mrs. Stinchcomb, Mrs. Dennison and Mrs. Robinson will be visiting the classes at Thomas School telling stories and talking about books.

SCHOOL MENU   Mon.-Chile, Hard Roll & Butter, Peanut Butter Cookie, Fruit, Milk
Tues.-Hot Dog, Broccoli or Corn, Pickle Chips, Strawberry Shortcake,Milk
Wed.-Turkey on a Bun, Tomato Soup, Peach, Chocolate Chip Cookie, Milk
Thurs.-Hamburger, Buttered Corn, Celery & Carrot Sticks, Cherries on
       Vanilla Pudding, Milk
Fri.-Ravioli & Meat Sauce, Tossed Salad, French Bread & Butter,
       Ice Cream, Milk

5/4/73

APPENDIX G

CITIZENS ADVISORY COMMITTEE
CONSTITUTION

I. **General Objective**

The purpose of the Citizens Advisory Committee is to encourage and develop a high level of public interest and knowledge pertaining to school matters so as to maintain throughout the school district the highest standards of public school education.

This group will not in any way infringe upon administrative or Board of Education functions and duties, or attempt to dictate the formation of school policies.

The major function of this committee shall be to serve in a liaison capacity between the public, the Board of Education, and school administration. This function is to be achieved by the following methods:

a. To promote a better and broader understanding among the public of the policies, plans and actions of the Board of Education and the school administration.

b. To solicit and study suggestions from the public and present those suggestions having merit to the appropriate persons and groups.

c. To study and secure public reaction to contemplated action of the board of education and to serve in an advisory capacity to the board upon its request.

d. To dispel rumors and replace misinformation with facts.

e. To study and evaluate any proposed school legislation (local, state, national) placed on the ballot for public approval, and to publicize the results of such studies.

f. To promote a high esprit de corps among the public, parents, students, teachers and officials of the school system.

II. **Organization of Committee**

A. MEMBERSHIP

Membership shall be composed of 24 members: eight from each of the three communities. Ex officio members to be included in the meetings are:

One member or alternate representing the P. T. A. Council, up to two ex-officio members from the official teacher representative group, one member representing the school administration.

The 24 area members are to be selected by the remaining members of each one of the three areas, whenever a vacancy occurs in their area and approved by the Executive Committee. The members shall serve for a two-year term under an annual rotation plan, in which the term of office of one-half of the members expires on June 30 each year. Insofar as possible, successors shall be appointed to represent the widest possible geographic coverage from each area. In selecting new members, recommendations of community and school leaders shall be sought. A diversity of membership shall also be sought, particularly to insure representation of both youth and senior citizens. Representatives whose terms expire are eligible for reappointment.

If a member misses three (3) consecutive meetings without a valid excuse acceptable to the executive committee or without having an alternate attend for him, the member will be dropped.

B. CHAIRMAN

The chairman shall be nominated annually by the Executive Committee. Additional nomination may be made from the floor. The chairman shall then be elected by the general committee. This election shall be held just prior to the expiration of the existing chairman's term. A chairman may be re-elected for more than one term of office.

The chairman shall appoint a recording secretary for the general committee. He shall also appoint a treasurer.

The term of service shall be from July 1 to June 30 of the succeeding year.

C. GENERAL COMMITTEE

At the beginning of each term the general committee shall form subcommittees for specific purposes. Nonmembers of the general committee may be invited to serve on the subcommittees. Each community shall be represented on each subcommittee. A chairman and a recording secretary shall be elected by each subcommittee.

D. EXECUTIVE COMMITTEE

The Executive Committee shall consist of the chairmen of the subcommittees, the chairman of the general committee, and a representative of the school administration. The chairman of the general committee shall serve as chairman of the executive committee.

E. MEETINGS

The general committee shall meet monthly.

All meetings of the general committee will be open to the public and regular meetings will be announced in local newspapers.

Special meetings of the general committee will be called whenever necessary by the Chairman.

Subcommittees shall meet as specific needs indicate.

The Executive Committee will meet monthly. Special meetings may be called by the Chairman.

F. DUTIES OF MEMBERS

1. Attend regular meetings in order to become apprised of school matters, so as to be able to act in everyday life as an authoritative source of information and to serve as a channel for the dissemination of facts.

2. Members of the Citizens Advisory Committee shall be urged to be well informed on the actions of the Board of Education through attendance at Board meetings or through study of Board reports.

3. The school administration shall be urged to assist in acquainting members of the administrative staff and members of the Board of Education with Citizens Advisory Committee members.

APPENDIX H

SUMMARY — SUPERINTENDENT'S ADVISORY COMMITTEE

 # THE EXCHANGE

A PUBLICATION OF THE SUPERINTENDENT'S ADVISORY COMMITTEE
XENIA CITY SCHOOLS, XENIA, OHIO 45385

As this was the last formal meeting of the year, we spent some time in circumspect and tried to list our accomplishments for the year, as well as some ideas which we initiated that still deserve additional consideration or study.

Accomplishments:

1. Kindergarten Parent Conferences were scheduled for the end of the first semester rather than during the fall parent conference period.

2. A policy for substitute teachers:

    (a) Maintain the same hours as regular teachers.
    (b) Make a written report for the regular teachers.

3. A 1:15 p.m. dismissal time for parent conference days.

Clarification:

1. Title I equipment may be made available to any teacher when it is not being used by the Title I Program.

2. A request for a job description for custodians was made.

3. Circulating the certificate requirements for the professional and permanent teaching certificates.

Recommended for Study:

1. A new non-letter grade card for all elementary schools.

2. A nine-week grading period.

3. An exam-week for junior and senior high schools; students should only report for exams.

The Superintendent's Advisory Committee will meet next year at the request of Mr. William West, the new superintendent. All schools who have had a representative on this committee who has served for two years, are asked to elect a replacement for next year. The others that have served one year are asked to serve their second year.

Mary Zambon
Recorder

APPENDIX I

COMMUNITY SEMINAR DISCUSSION GUIDE (SAMPLE PAGE)

Questions:

(Write your answer under the question. In the box to the left, rank it 1, 2 or 3 in importance according to the judgment of the majority of the group.)

☐ 1. While approximately 60% of last year's graduates are in college or in some special training program, the remaining may not be prepared to carry on a productive life in the future. Should the high school expand its program to give more specialized training to this group of students?

☐ 2. The increase in the number of pupils enrolled in Individual Assistance in the past six years has called for an increase in classrooms, specially trained teachers, and special materials. Should this program continue to be expanded in accordance with need?

☐ 3. The projected enrollment for the next five years for the Xenia schools as a whole, is leveling off. However, a pronounced increase is forecast at the high school level. What plans should be made to take care of this increase in the secondary school?

☐ 4. Drop-outs are a serious problem. Xenia Schools experience a 30% drop-out rate.

    a.   How can drop-outs be prevented?

    b.   What can be done to enable drop-outs to become substantial, self-supporting citizens in this day when a college education is very important?

☐ 5. Would it be desirable to eliminate certain courses to provide additional funds?

    6.   Other remarks:

APPENDIX J

ONE PAGE QUESTIONNAIRE

Take this
opportunity to GRADE US !

Please rate our school services and/or programs
by checking your opinions of our performance. Your comments
and suggestions are welcomed. Thank you!

SCHOOL SERVICES and PROGRAMS

Type of Program (Please check)

	RATING		
	Good	Fair	Poor
☐ Individual Parent-School Administrator Conference	☐	☐	☐
☐ Individual Parent-Teacher Conference	☐	☐	☐
☐ Informational Meeting	☐	☐	☐
☐ Orientation Program	☐	☐	☐
☐ Educational Speaker	☐	☐	☐
☐ Panel Discussion	☐	☐	☐
☐ Psychological Service	☐	☐	☐
☐ School Open House	☐	☐	☐
☐ Student Performance	☐	☐	☐
☐ Counseling Service	☐	☐	☐
☐ Other (please describe)_____			

_____

_____

Name of School:_____ Location:_____

Date:_____

	Yes	No
Did your problem or concern receive prompt, courteous attention?	☐	☐
Were you satisfied that proper preparation had been made for this program or service?	☐	☐
Were your questions answered reasonably and satisfactorily?	☐	☐
Did you receive the information you hoped to receive by participating in this program or service?	☐	☐

We'd appreciate your suggestions for improving this program or service._____

_____

_____

Other comments regarding school services, programs, personnel, curriculum, etc.:_____

_____

_____

_____

_____

APPENDIX K

SCHOOL QUESTIONNAIRE

Answering this poll – ☐ Father ☐ Mother ☐ Both

1. I have children enrolled in grades –
   (circle)

   K 1 2 3 4 5 6 7 8 9 10 11 12

2. We have lived in Wellesley for –
   (circle)

   1 2 3 4 5 6 More years

3. I am generally – ☐ very pleased
   ☐ satisfied ☐ dissatisfied with my
   children's schools.

   Comment _____

4. The instruction which my children have
   received has been –

   ☐ superior ☐ good ☐ adequate ☐ poor

   Comment _____

5. It is my opinion that the activities and experiences designed to supplement the basic studies,
   provide enrichment and broaden the scope of the curriculum have been:

Activity	Excellent	Adequate	Poor	Too frequent	Infrequent
Assembly programs					
Club activities					
Student government					
Field trips					
Student publications					
School library					
Recreational activities					
Social activities					
Cultural activities					
Comment					

6. I feel that the program offered my child in the following subject areas is:

(please check)

	Excellent	Good	Adequate	Inadequate
Math				
Science				
For. Lang. (secondary school)				
Home Ec. (secondary school)				
English				
Social Studies				
Reading				
Ind. Arts (secondary school)				
Music				
Art				
Phys. Ed.				
Other				

Explain briefly why you have checked any subject "inadequate."

7. My child has used the special services of
   the following –

   ☐ Remedial Reading ☐ Speech correction
   ☐ Guidance Activities and Services
   ☐ Other

   We have been very pleased satisfied dissatisfied with thes special help our child has been receiving.

   Comment _____

8. From the point of view of their frequency
   and effectiveness, please rank the following
   items which are designed to provide you
   with information regarding the school, its
   activities and your child's progress –

   E-Excellent G-Good F-Fair P-Poor Grade

   Report Cards _____
   News releases concerning
   schools in TOWNSMAN _____
   YOUR SCHOOLS _____
   Annual School Report _____
   Scheduled Parent-Teacher
   Conferences _____
   School Radio Broadcasts _____
   P.T.A. _____
   Special school programs
   for parents _____
   Others _____
   Please explain why you marked any of the
   above with "F" or "P" and how you
   would suggest improving these items. _____

   _____

9. I think the schools might consider the
   following in working to improve their
   instructional programs _____

   _____

10. Any other constructive suggestions or com-
    ments will be greatly appreciated.

11. What is the one thing about the Wellesley
    schools which you like the best?
    What is the one thing about the Wellesley
    school which you dislike most?

12. NOTE: Only parents of Junior and High
    School students are requested to answer
    the following.
    Are you satisfied with the facilities, ar-
    rangements, schedule, cost, regulations,
    etc., of the school lunch program.

    ☐ Yes ☐ No ☐ Uncertain

    Comment _____

13. As a parent I feel that the banking oppor-
    tunity provided children at school should
    be –

    ☐ Continued ☐ Discontinued

    Comment _____

14. Do you feel that the banking opportunity
    should start in grade 2?

    ☐ Yes ☐ No

    Comment _____

    We greatly appreciate your taking the time
    and effort to assist us by filling out this
    questionnaire.

    (Not required)

    Name _____

    Address _____

APPENDIX L

SCHOOL QUESTIONNAIRE

WARRENSVILLE HEIGHTS CITY SCHOOLS
Community Census

In order to plan for the future of our schools we are calling upon each of you to complete this form. I will appreciate it very much if you could take the time to complete this community census sheet and have it ready for the census enumerator who will call upon you during the week of March 8 to 13.

All of the questions are directed to the head of the household. No name, however, should be written on this sheet. It will be placed in a common envelope by the enumerator and your anonymity is assured.

Sincerely,

	Yes	No	Amount
1. The following questions refer to school attendance. Please answer each part. (Please Mark X in the appropriate Blocks)			
A. Do you have any children attending the Warrensville City Schools? If yes, how many? A-			
B. Do you have any children attending elsewhere in grades kindergarten through twelve? If yes, how many? B-			
C. Do you have children of pre-school age in your household? If yes, how many? C-			
D. Do you have any children in college? If yes, how many? D-			
Did these children you have attending college graduate from Warrensville Heights Senior High School? D-			

	Own	Rent	
2. Do you live in: Indicate type with an X in appropriate black			
1. Single Family Unit 1.			
2. Multiple Family Unit (One bedroom) 2.			
3. Multiple Family Unit (Two bedroom) 3.			
4. Multiple Family Unit (Three bedroom) 4.			
5. Trailer Unit 5.			

	X	
3. Occupaotioal Areas: Indicate with an X.		
1. Professional and Managerial 1.		
2. Clerical and Sales 2.		
3. Skilled 3.		
4. Semi-Skilled 4.		
5. Un-Skilled 5.		
6. Retired 6.		

	X	
4. Highest level of Schooling Completed: Indicate with an X		
1. Completed Elementary 1.		
2. Attended High School 2.		
3. Completed High School 3.		
4. Attended College 4.		
5. Completed College 5.		

	No.	
5. Please react to the following questions below by writing the number (appropriate to the response in the scale) in the Answer Block 1. - Very much 2. - Much 3. - Some 4. - Little 5. - Very little		
A. To what extent is there good communication between school and the home in the Warrensville Heights School System? A A-		
B. To what extent do you think this community will support additional tax money for schools? B-		
C. To what extent are our schools teaching the basic skills? Reading, writing, arithmetic, etc. C-		
D. To what extent do you feel that our schools are preparing young people for college or post-high school employment? D-		

Be sure that each question has been answered.

APPENDIX M

SCHOOL QUESTIONNAIRE

ONE MOMENT PLEASE . . .

That's all it will take to answer these questions. In order to improve our efforts to keep you fully aware of school policies and programs, we need your help. Won't you take a moment, now, to fill in this questionnaire and mail it promptly? It will help us to return the favor and provide information you would like to have about your school system. Just fold it and drop it in the nearest mailbox. THANK YOU!

1. In general, how do you feel about the education children are receiving in the Hudson Public Schools?

    Excellent _____   Fair _____
    Good _____   Poor _____

2. In what ways could school operation be improved?

3. What are the main sources of your information about the schools?

    (Please number in order of importance 1, 2, 3, etc.)

    Your children _____   Akron Beacon Journal _____
    Neighbors _____   School Newsletter, the "Report Card" _____
    School Personnel _____   Other Sources (please name) _____
    Hudson Times _____

4. Do you feel that you receive enough information about the schools to be well informed?

    Yes _____   No _____

    Please check areas in which you would like more information:

    Subjects Studied _____   Grading and Testing _____
    Buildings and Grounds _____   Financial Data _____
    Teachers and Administration _____ Guidance _____
    Rules and Regulations _____   Pupil Achievement _____
    Extracurricular Activities _____ Other (please name) _____

5. How long have you lived in Hudson?____ years

6. How many school-age children are in your family?_____
   In what grades? Circle each grade: K - 1 - 2 - 3 - 4 - 5 - 6 - 7 - 8 - 9 - 10 - 11 - 12

7. Please check the school activities you regularly attend:

    Open Houses _____   Parent Meetings _____
    PTO Meetings _____   Athletic Events _____
    Plays or Musicals _____

Any comments would be appreciated: